PREDATOR

D0332769

PREDATOR

The true story of Levi Bellfield, the
man who murdered Milly Dowler, Marsha
McDonnell and Amelie Delagrange

JOHN McSHANE

JOHN BLAKE

Published by John Blake Publishing Ltd,
3 Bramber Court, 2 Bramber Road,
London W14 9PB, England

www.johnblakepublishing.co.uk

www.facebook.com/Johnblakepub   facebook

twitter.com/johnblakepub   twitter

First published in paperback in 2011

ISBN: 9781843586739

British Library Cataloguing-in-Publication Data:

A catalogue record for this book is available from the British Library.

Design by www.envydesign.co.uk

Printed and bound by CPI Group (UK) Ltd, Croydon, CR0 4YY

1 3 5 7 9 10 8 6 4 2

Papers used by John Blake Publishing are natural, recyclable products made
from wood grown in sustainable forests. The manufacturing processes
conform to the environmental regulations of the country of origin.

PROLOGUE

It would be hard to find three more typically English scenes: a shaded patch of ground in the heart of a Hampshire wood where the sun struggles to penetrate the canopy of the trees, a cricket pitch preserved for years amid encroaching suburban sprawl and a quiet street of Victorian homes merging slowly into post-war houses on the outskirts of London. A trio so enticing, so comforting and above all so safe that they could have been photographed and used in a tourist-board brochure as embodying all that is good, right and decent about this 'green and pleasant land'.

Yet, it was here that their young bodies were found – the 13-year-old schoolgirl whose disappearance shocked a nation, a young woman who had left her home in France to journey to a country that she loved in order to help her master English, and a

19-year-old gap-year student walking home late at night. They all shared the same fate.

All were to be victims of a man they did not know, who did not know them, yet who was to end their lives with acts of violent savagery that no normal, decent human being could comprehend. A brute of a man whose victims were chosen at random. No reason, no cause, no provocation of any sort, no matter how mild or innocent, had led them to their fate. They just happened to be in the wrong place at the wrong time.

Unwittingly and innocently, they had entered into the nightmare that was the world of Levi Bellfield, a man so twisted that decency and morality, the boundaries of right and wrong, did not exist for him. He cared for himself and no others. He brought devastation into the lives of all he encountered, a violent, escalating mayhem that knew no boundaries, no limit.

Whether his victims were close to him or they had never met, it mattered not. All their lives suffered from the impact of his savagery. Some survived, some did not, but no one – including the relatives of those he brutalised – escaped the devastating effect of an encounter with the six-foot, overweight bully that was Bellfield.

The deaths of Milly Dowler, Marsha McDonnell and Amelie Delagrange were shocking and, as such, generated a vast amount of media coverage. The manner of their dying, the discovery of their bodies and the massive, lengthy hunt for the killer, ensured events were followed closely by newspapers and television channels around the world. The subsequent arrest and trials of

Bellfield meant this level of interest continued and the aftermath of some of the most remarkable courtroom scenes ever seen, even at the Old Bailey – a court which in its history has witnessed many major confrontations – were to take on a political and moral aspect reaching far beyond its boundaries.

Bellfield's trial in connection with Milly Dowler was to be especially provocative, as were the events and recriminations at its conclusion. They will be dealt with in detail in this book but it would be wrong to infer from that analysis that more 'importance' is attached to her death than the other two young women who perished at Bellfield's hands. In no way can the impact and nature of the grief that he generated be calculated or in any gruesome sense 'rated'. Nor, indeed, does it illustrate any diminution in the gravity of the impact Bellfield had on others, whose encounters with him had a lasting effect on their lives. Unlike Milly, Marsha and Amelie, they may have lived, but they too paid a price, albeit of a different nature.

Bellfield was a predator, and, like all his kind, he focused on those who were weaker than he, more vulnerable, unlikely and, indeed, unable to strike back. As the man who twice led the prosecution case against him at the Old Bailey, Mr Brian Altman QC, so accurately and chillingly put it, he truly was 'Every parent's nightmare'.

CHAPTER 1

The day started normally for Milly Dowler and her family, a busy Thursday in the middle of a hectic school week. Milly made sure that her father Bob gave her a breakfast-time kiss. He had innocently neglected to kiss the 13-year-old, his youngest daughter, the previous day because he had left home early so he was happy to make amends. 'It was a bit of a family habit that I gave her a kiss in the morning,' he said.

The Dowler family had two cars, a blue Peugeot 206 and a red VW Golf estate, and Bob Dowler planned to take the estate with him to a business meeting not far from their home in Walton-on-Thames in Surrey.

Normally, IT expert Bob would not return home until between 6.30pm and 7.00pm, but as the meeting was in nearby Basingstoke he said he would probably be back by about 4.00pm.

He didn't leave until about 9.45am and, around 3.00–3.10pm, he returned to the comfortable, detached family house that had been their home for nine years, earlier than he originally planned. The Dowlers were having some work carried out on the house and it was the builders' first day on the job but they had left by then.

In the normal course of events, such trivial timings would be inconsequential. Yet, by that evening – and in the years to follow – the hours and minutes of that terrible day, 21 March 2002, would be analysed, examined and argued over in the full glare of national and international spotlights. Exactly who was where and at what time was to become of pivotal importance. But all that was still in the future and, mercifully, none of the Dowler family could foresee the horrors that lay in store.

Bob and his wife Sally had met in October 1981 and married two and a half years later. In January 1986, their elder daughter Gemma was born, and on 25 June 1988 another daughter, Amanda, known to everyone as Milly, was born. Sally taught mathematics at Heathside School in Weybridge, where her two daughters were both pupils, and the normal routine was that their mother would drive them to school. Mother and daughters laughed as they listened to the Chris Tarrant show on the Peugeot's radio as the DJ humorously tried to arrange a blind-date for one of his on-air team.

That morning, Milly had a drama lesson in which, dressed in a dark blue-black tracksuit, she played a restaurant owner. In the course of that lesson, she spoke to her friends of her excitement at being at a Pop Idol concert on the Tuesday night when she had seen her favourite artist, Gareth Gates, perform. Milly had cried with pleasure at seeing him. The home video of Milly the Monday night before the concert, laughing and smiling while she ironed her jeans, the first time she had ever ironed anything, was later to be seen by millions, released in the hope that it might help find her.

It had been a busy week for Milly. At the weekend, she had taken part in a fun run with her uncle, Brian Gilbertson, who had only come into her life a few months earlier. It had only recently been revealed that her grandmother had given birth to him when she was 16. The happy day had ended with Milly playing the saxophone at the party afterwards.

During that Thursday morning break, Milly ate three packets of crisps and a chocolate muffin. Her friend Danielle Sykes, who was in the same Year 9 form as Milly, said to her jokingly that she was a pig for eating such food. Lessons included drama and science in the afternoon.

Milly had some artwork to finish at school and, as her mother had a tutorial after normal school ended in the afternoon at 2.55pm and Gemma was off to do trampoline exercise, the family would then all leave for home together. But Milly came to see her mother and said that she had done her work at lunchtime and did not want to wait around for a lift. She gave her mother her gym kit and told her she would catch the train from Weybridge instead. The girls were given £2.50 a day for lunch and 80p a day for the train by their parents.

This was the first of many accidents of fate that day which were to place Milly in the presence of the man who was to take her life. How could she or her mother know, how could anyone know that a small change in a mundane routine would have such consequences? No one was to blame; no one was at fault.

Milly walked out of school at 3.07pm wearing her school uniform: a short grey skirt, a white blouse and a light blue V-neck sweater. She had on her navy-blue school blazer with an emblem over the breast pocket and on her feet she had a small pair of white trainer socks and black Pod shoes. She was carrying a beige and black JanSport rucksack. In it were her schoolbooks, a pink Barbie pencil case and a red and white purse decorated with heart shapes, her house keys on a bottle-opener key ring and her Nokia 3210 mobile phone with her name. Around the young girl's wrist was a pink, beaded friendship bracelet.

She left school with her friends Danielle, Cara Dawson and Jacqueline Pignolly, and they walked to Weybridge railway station. At 3.23pm, she went on to the platform with Danielle. On the walk to the station, she had removed her sweater and put it in her bag.

The girls caught the 3.26pm scheduled train from Weybridge and, in the normal course of events, Milly would have stayed on board until it reached Hersham, the nearest station to her home. Instead, she decided to get off at the stop before Hersham, Walton, to have some chips with Danielle at the Travellers Cafe on the station platform. It was another one of those 'if only' decisions.

There were images of Milly later seen by millions as she left school and as she reached Weybridge. There was nothing from Walton station, however; a decorator had accidentally disconnected its CCTV during work he was carrying out.

Jacqueline stayed on the train and carried on until Hersham. Although Cara got off at Walton too, she immediately walked straight home on the route that Milly should have taken soon afterwards: down Station Avenue, across a road junction with traffic lights known as The Halfway and along Rydens Road, arriving home some five or ten minutes later.

Inside the cafe where Milly had decided to stay for chips were three boys from school: Christopher Price, Adam Raine and Miles Pink. Danielle had to lend Milly 10p to make sure that she had enough for the bag of chips and Milly used Christopher's mobile to call home, hers being out of credit. The Dowlers had a rule that if one of their daughters was going to be delayed then they should call their parents at home. The 26-second call was made at 3.47pm. Milly told her father that she had stopped for chips and would be home in about 30 minutes. She didn't ask for a lift and Bob didn't offer her one – there seemed to be no need. It was all so ordinary, so uneventful. A young daughter slightly delayed, a busy father reassured by her call.

Danielle Sykes had an elder sister, 17-year-old Natalie, who was studying at Esher College. She called and asked Danielle to wait for her as she was on her way from Esher to Walton station on the train.

When Natalie arrived at the station, she joined the others in the cafe run by brothers Anthony and Robert Stevens. After the chips had been consumed, the girls went their separate ways; the sisters going one way out of the station, Milly leaving as though to go towards Station Avenue.

Alongside the station was the business centre of Walton Tyre and Exhaust – later replaced by a modern Audi showroom – after the exit gate where the Sykes girls last saw Milly. That too was to change in the years that followed, being replaced by a barrier. An old bicycle shelter stood there, again to be updated in the years after Milly disappeared, and a telephone kiosk was nearby, also subsequently removed. However, some vital features of the area remained. The entrances to the station car park on the southern side of Station Avenue were unaltered and, most importantly, the position of a bus stop on the northern side remained the same.

Milly was seen in Station Avenue by Katherine Laynes, 15, also a Heathside pupil, albeit in Year 11 and a friend of Gemma Dowler. She had met Millie as she had recently been to a birthday party for Gemma and she had also seen the younger sister at school. She therefore recognised Milly as she walked on the south side of Station Avenue and the two girls made eye contact. Katherine was at the bus stop on the northern side of the road and she lost sight of Milly as her view was obstructed by an advertising hoarding at one end of the stop. If Milly had stayed on the south side of the road, she would have walked past the striking

Birds Eye building, a three-storey, 1960s office block which had become Grade II listed.

Katherine boarded her bus and once on board looked for Milly but could not see her; she had vanished. Milly had gone, as an Old Bailey jury was to hear years later, 'in the blink of an eye'. She was never seen alive again – except by her killer.

The exact events and timings involved in this last journey of Milly's and her snack with friends will be analysed in detail later on in this book; the where, when and how of her disappearance forming a major part of the trial Levi Bellfield was to face for her murder nine years on. The events in the Dowler house prior to Milly's disappearance will also be examined, as will what took place that terrible afternoon and discoveries that were made in subsequent days and weeks. They were distressing in the details that they revealed and, importantly, even more controversial in the manner they became public.

Bob Dowler, then 50, was still at the family's Walton Park home as that March afternoon gave way to early evening. He had gone into the drawing room at the front of the house that he used as his study and had been on a number of telephone calls he was to later say were 'stressful'. The door to the room was closed.

He had arranged to go out that night at about 7.00pm with a friend to a concert in Guildford and Sally, 42, was to babysit for relatives who were going out to celebrate their anniversary. Sally came into the room and gave him a post-it note reading, 'I'm off to Pete's, where's Milly?'

By the time he had finished his call, there was only Gemma in the house and she told him that Milly was not at home. She had arrived and called out, 'Amanda, Amanda, where are you?' and received no reply.

At 5.21pm, Bob phoned Milly's mobile and left a message to the effect of, 'Where are you? Mum's gone out, I'm going out at 7.00pm. Where are you?' Then he made calls to Danielle Sykes and also to his wife, twice, to let her know what was happening.

Bob Dowler went out in his car to look for his younger daughter. There was no sign of her. He telephoned the local hospitals without success. At 7.07pm, he rang Addlestone police station in Surrey and 'pretty quickly' police were at the house, he said. In fact, they arrived just three minutes later, at 7.10pm. Bob, Sally and Gemma were all at home by now, as were Sally's nephews. The officers were allowed in Milly's room which they described at the time as 'a normal teenager's room. It was messy and untidy and the bed was unmade.'

The police went to Walton station, spoke with Cara Dawson and Danielle Sykes, carried out searches between the station and Milly's home between 9.05pm and 10.10pm, and returned to the Dowler home several times that night.

Then the officers filed a missing person report. The hunt for Milly Dowler had begun.

CHAPTER 2

The weekend of 23 March 2002 saw the first appearance of stories in the national media and television about the disappearance of a 13-year-old girl on her way home from school. Milly Dowler was to become synonymous with the fears of parents everywhere for children's wellbeing and safety in a twisted world.

The hope that fraught Saturday and Sunday was that she was all right. It was not, of course, to be the case.

Her uncle Brian Gilbertson had been out the night of her disappearance with homemade posters of his niece and that weekend they were pinned or wrapped around trees and lampposts on the route she should have taken home and in the surrounding districts.

The news of Milly's disappearance brought back for some the

memories of another case that had ended in tragedy, that of Sarah Payne, the eight-year-old girl abducted and killed during a visit to West Sussex two years earlier who had grown up in Hersham less than a mile from the Dowler family home.

More than a hundred police officers joined the search for Milly, aided by dogs and a fire brigade boat-team. They combed allotments, fields, waterways and bushes for clues. Concerned members of the public joined in and a helicopter with thermal-imaging equipment flew over the area, while divers searched nearby River Mole.

Bob Dowler said, 'We've been absolutely overwhelmed by everybody's help and support. It's my wife's birthday this week – it would be the best present in the world if we got her home safe. Someone, somewhere must know something. Any suggestion, however small, could be vital.'

Referring to the phone call he had received from Milly while she was at Walton station, he said, 'She told me where she was, who she was with, and said she was going to be home in half an hour … and I said, "That is quite all right, darling." We have lived in the area for a number of years. We have always felt comfortable. If I had been at all concerned, I would have gone to the station and picked her up.'

Sally Dowler appeared with her husband at a press conference at Staines police station that weekend. Looking into the cameras, she said, 'We're devastated. We're just so desperately worried. Please, please give her back to us. The only thing that keeps us going is to think that she's out there and that we're going to get her back. Milly, if you are watching or listening to this, we want you to know that we all love you and miss you very much and can't wait to have you back home with us.' Her daughter was a happy student, she said, and she mentioned Milly playing her saxophone at a charity reception and the Pop Idol concert.

Will Young, winner of *Pop Idol*, had performed that night too. He added his voice to the appeal: 'Amanda, please go home or contact your family. They are missing you and are very worried. Also, do it for me and all the other *Pop Idol* fans.'

The headteacher at Heathside School was Glyn Willoughby. He said the entire community was working to find the girl: 'We are assisting the police and Amanda's family as much as we can and our thoughts are with them at this time. We are hoping there will be good news. We are doing everything possible to attain a happy result from this very traumatic and difficult situation for all involved. The entire community is really in limbo at the moment, wanting to know what more they can do.'

By that Monday, 25 March, hundreds of people were either out searching for Milly or distributing and displaying posters on buildings throughout Walton-on-Thames. It was the first day of the school holiday but many of Milly's pals and schoolmates were among those helping. Those children who had been on outings or shopping trips were met by their anxious parents as they left Walton station rather than going home on their own – no one was taking any chances.

Superintendent Alan Sharp, the police officer leading the hunt, admitted that his officers were 'no further forward' in their efforts to trace her. 'We remain extremely concerned for Amanda's safety. It seems astonishing that a young girl could have vanished in broad daylight in an area like this,' said Superintendent Sharp, the operations commander for north Surrey. 'Someone must have seen her and that is our one hope. At the moment we are no further forward.'

He said the investigation was still a missing person inquiry, but admitted that abduction had not been ruled out. 'We want to know if anyone saw her get into a car or stopping to talk to anyone,' said Sharp. 'Her parents, friends and all her family share our great concern now that so much time has passed. But we are not ruling out that Amanda may be watching, listening to or reading this appeal and, if she is, we want her to contact her parents immediately or contact the police and tell us where she is. We have done extensive searches over a wide area but we are no further forward in finding her.'

An actress, 17-year-old Elizabeth Pryor, retraced the last known steps of Milly in a reconstruction of her disappearance shown on that week's *Crimewatch* on BBC. Superintendent Sharp said, 'We are extremely frustrated. Having disappeared on a busy road, it is astonishing no one has seen her if she had been abducted. We are hopeful of finding her alive but, as each day passes, it becomes more difficult. We would have expected to have something after six days. It's disturbing.' Bob, Sally and Gemma were all at the family home as the search continued, he said. 'It is very traumatic for them. Given the circumstances, they are bearing up extremely well.'

One theory being put forward to explain Milly's disappearance was that she could have a secret boyfriend. But her friend Hannah McDonald from Chertsey, also 13, said, 'She definitely hasn't run away but I'm keeping my hopes up that she has. She has no boyfriend, no secret boyfriend and no secret friends. I'd have known about it if she had. On the Friday night there was a gang of us going to a disco at a school in Chertsey. She was going to tell the boy she fancied there how she felt about him. Milly had already told his best friend and she was really looking forward to it. She wouldn't get into a car without knowing the person unless she was grabbed. She would have been too scared to put up a fight.'

Milly received her school report shortly before she disappeared but Hannah said it hadn't been anything to worry about. 'She wasn't down. She was messing about with the boys she sat next to – just being Milly. It wasn't a bad report. It said something about homework and chattiness in class. She's not bad, just cheeky.'

The 28th of March was Sally Dowler's 43rd birthday. It was an agonising day for her and her family, and she put her anguish in words when she said, 'Somebody must know where she is, whatever has happened to her. I can't rest because I can't think what's happened to her. I would like to think that she has run away because that might be a way that we would get her back, but

I can't think of any reason why she would want to run away. Please come home, darling.'

Bob said, 'It would be the best present in the world if we got Milly home safe. If she sees all the coverage she must be thinking, What have I done? The message we want to say to her is, "You haven't done anything wrong." If you can make that step to come home to us and call us, it's absolutely fine. We are not cross. You can see we are upset so come home please.' But he admitted abduction was 'one of the most logical possibilities'. And he pleaded, 'Give her back to us so she can be back with the family. I hope to God if that person is listening and watching, they will find it in themselves to look at us and understand what this is doing.'

That same day, a large team of forensic officers began a thorough search of the family home. Surrey police said that its 26 officers had gone in with an 'open mind' about what they would find in detailed chemical analysis of the contents of the house and garden. They had the full co-operation of Amanda's parents, who were not being treated as suspects. Six police vans moved in and taped off access to the front and back of the house in Walton-on-Thames after the family left for the filming of *Crimewatch UK* in London.

The officers spent much of the day scouring both the Dowlers' home and also land close to where Amanda was last sighted. After cordoning off the £350,000 property, they were seen with spades in the back garden, examining drains and picking through nearby allotments, gardens, streams and culverts. Three plastic boxes were removed from the house after the search and police said the forensic investigation could last several days.

Police had already conducted an initial search of the house three days after Milly went missing. They had taken DNA samples from personal items, such as her toothbrush and hairbrush, and searched for 'relevant' personal effects. During the second search, the youngster's bedroom was the centre of the hunt which began at lunchtime. Officers inspected and removed notebooks, diaries and other material. At about 4.00pm, boiler-suited forensic investigators were seen carrying out three boxes the size of milk crates. These were loaded into a white Vauxhall Astra van.

The family's two cars were also minutely searched. 'The investigation has still not given any great developments and therefore it is absolutely vital that we go back to the house,' explained Superintendent Sharp. 'It remains the most fertile ground for possible clues as to where Amanda may be or why she has disappeared.' He stressed that officers would not be digging in the garden and explained the search was concentrating on documents and other items that may give some clue to Milly's whereabouts. 'It may be that something that was insignificant last time is now significant.'

A Surrey police spokesman added, 'We waited until the family left for the day because it's more convenient for them and us.' The force said the Dowlers were not expected home until after the search was completed, which could take another two days. Police were also questioning passengers at Walton-on-Thames railway station because it was exactly a week since her disappearance and they were hopeful of coming across people who had been there at the time.

Despite more than a thousand calls from the public, there had been no positive leads. Intensive searches of railway lines, reservoirs and fields, involving scores of officers, helicopters and aerial photographs, had failed to yield any clues. The CCTV cameras on top of the Birds Eye office block in Station Avenue had also been examined. They failed to pick up any images of Milly walking homewards but they too were to figure in the eventual trial of Bellfield. One report at the time noted 'police are continuing house-to-house enquiries on a nearby council estate. Detectives have already made checks on local sex offenders and are examining whether the disappearance may be linked to any others.'

Countless doors were knocked on, but there was no response from the one that Bellfield had no doubt taken his young victim to. On no fewer than ten occasions police knocked without reply on the door of 24 Collingwood Place, a ground-floor flat in a small, modern block, just yards from Station Avenue. It was only when a new occupant had moved in on the eleventh occasion police visited that they had a reply. By then, Levi Bellfield and the traces of his crime were long gone. The failure to link him to that flat at that time was to be one of the complaints levelled at Surrey police in the future.

What was to be discovered in the Dowler house, however,

among the possessions not only of Milly but of her father, were also major issues in the trial that was to take place some nine years later. The intimate details of a young girl's writings and the embarrassing nature of the objects belonging to Bob Dowler were eventually to be revealed.

Gemma Dowler wrote a letter, an open one, in which she poured out her heart over Milly's disappearance, appealing to anyone who might have taken her: 'Please return her safely. I am missing her very much. The nights are the worst,' Gemma wrote. 'My imagination runs wild thinking about what has happened to her. Every day I wake up with the hope that Milly will return. My life has been turned upside down.' The letter was written on ordinary writing paper in a girl's tiny hand, decorated with hearts, stars and kisses, with 'I Love U Milly' drawn inside a big heart at the bottom. 'If someone has taken Milly, please return her safely to us as I am missing her very much and I couldn't wish for a lovelier sister.'

Gemma told how Milly had been planning to help her get ready for a prom at Heathside School and Milly was going to share her excitement by going around the shops with her and flicking through the dress rails. 'One week ago, I was looking forward to the Easter holidays. Milly was going to come shopping with me to choose my prom dress and we had planned a great big Easter party.'

Sally explained the significance of the prom: 'Gemma has her GCSEs coming up and the end of school prom. It was a really big deal and Milly was going to come out with Gemma and myself to choose a beautiful dress for it.'

The Dowlers had also bought family tickets for *My Fair Lady* in the West End. The star of the musical, Jonathan Pryce, even made an appeal for Milly on what would have been the day of the Dowlers' visit to the theatre.

So distressing had it all become for Milly's mother there were even times when, momentarily, Sally forgot that her daughter was missing. 'I woke up this morning and thought there was something she wanted for Easter – a tiny sports bag like a handbag. I thought for a moment, I've got to get that, and then my heart sank with a terrible feeling of foreboding. It's a living hell.'

Although both girls had their own bedrooms, Milly had moved in with Gemma late in the previous year 'They shared a bedroom. They've got their own bedrooms, but they shared one together through choice,' Bob explained.

In spite of the family concerns, Superintendent Sharp was widely quoted that last weekend in March, saying, 'We still believe she may have gone off on her own accord. If she did get into a car, it is more likely it would have been with someone she knew. All of the material we have obtained in statement form or otherwise is enabling us to build up a picture of Amanda as a person, what her relations with people were, to get a clue as to where she may have gone and what her motivation may have been and whether she was closer to one person more than any others.'

He said the inquiry had been 'deluged' with calls from the

public but there had been no evidence of Milly struggling with any kidnapper. 'It therefore leaves us to conclude that it is much more likely that Amanda has gone with someone she knows rather than being taken by force and abducted off the street.' He insisted, however, that all lines of inquiry were still open.

Two weeks after Milly vanished, Danielle Sykes, the friend she had stopped to have chips with, also made an appeal to her pal. 'You mean so much to so many people. You always manage to make me smile when I'm down and you are there for me if I want to talk. I love you, Milly, and I want you to be here with us. I have been remembering the times we have been together, little things that have stuck in my head: the song that we made together at the park with you on your saxophone and me singing. You could hardly play for laughing.' Danielle ended by saying, 'Please get in contact with someone. I have my mobile on so any time soon, just call. No one is angry with you; we just want you to return home. Love always.'

The hunt for Milly generated nationwide publicity and *Crimewatch* aroused particular interest and compassion. There were also several sightings of Milly, all of which were, of course, false. A stream at Malden Manor, Surrey, about seven miles from Walton, was searched by divers for two days after reports of a body being spotted in it. The National Missing Persons Helpline launched a campaign for both Milly and nine other, long-term missing children, featuring their faces on the sides of a fleet of lorries owned by Ford.

Seventeen days after Milly disappeared, one of the first public criticisms of the police investigation was aired, when a former detective constable with Surrey police told the *Sunday Telegraph*, 'They don't seem to have a clue what has happened to her.' The officer had worked on the case of a 16-year-old girl who, like Milly, had vanished. Six years earlier, the other teenager had disappeared from Dorking, not far from Walton. 'The search was just not done well enough … There was also a lack of sufficient house-to-house enquiries and numbers of people were not spoken to until later on. These were fundamental errors.' His comments were to be remarkably prescient.

Surrey police said they were doing everything they could to find Milly, a spokesman saying, 'From the outset, we have treated this case as a critical incident. We are following all lines of enquiry and not discounting any options at this stage. Since she went missing we have invested significant resources in the investigation. On any one day we have had more than a hundred officers working on the case.'

Images of Milly were already embedded in the public mind when police issued shots from the CCTV footage of her leaving her 1,300-pupil school on 21 March and at Weybridge station soon afterwards.

On Monday, 8 April, pupils returned to Heathside after the Easter break. 'Milly sits near me and there was this empty space,' one of her classmates said. 'That made people upset not to see her there. But the teacher immediately moved one boy into Amanda's seat so there was not this big hole. Her best friends spent the day trying to be cheerful, but I saw at least two really upset.'

As the pupils streamed through the school gates, they were greeted by the sight of three police officers, a waiting press pack and the news that two psychologists provided by the local education authority were on call to help staff and pupils. The educational psychologists had counselled Bell Farm Junior School in Hersham, where the sister and one of the brothers of murdered eight-year-old Sarah Payne were pupils.

Amanda's classmate said, 'A notice was read out in form-time at 8.45am from Mr Willoughby, telling us what had happened and saying he knows how upset we must be but to try and get on with our work. He said that if anyone feels upset or feels the need to talk to somebody about Amanda then there are special people in the school who can help us. Nobody thinks Amanda has run away. She was far too happy. In fact, I have never seen her unhappy. She was always laughing and singing. Everybody knows she has not run off so we don't really talk about what might have happened. Nobody can face talking about that. I last spoke to her on the day she disappeared. We were talking about *Pop Idol*, and who was nicer, Gareth or Will. We both decided Gareth.' Milly had been so excited at the concert that she had told sister Gemma that she thought Gareth was 'to die for'.

Mr Willoughby himself said, 'We are very distressed by Amanda's disappearance and are hoping and praying that she will be found safe and well as soon as possible.'

During that day, three six-strong teams from Surrey police widened their search between the school and Milly's home and scoured woodland south of the A317 and scrubland near Weybridge's Elmbridge Leisure Centre. By this time, there had been an astonishing 2,200 calls in to the police about her disappearance.

Gemma did not attend school that first day back but did soon return and was then interviewed by presenter Becky Jago for the BBC's *Newsround* programme. She was accompanied to the west London studios by her parents and the show was broadcast after *Blue Peter*. It is worth repeating in length for the insight it gives into the bond between the sisters and the distress that Milly's disappearance had caused.

Q What's Milly like as a sister?

A She's really nice, she's really pretty, she's got a lovely personality. She's funny. She's a great laugh if you ever need cheering up or anything.

Q What do you think is the most special thing about her?

A The girly chats we had when we shared a room. We always had them really late. We'd be reading each other's text messages and things like that. I'd find out about her boyfriends and everything.

Q What do you miss most about her?

A I think at night time, the girly chats. When you try to sleep you just can't get it out of your head. You keep thinking, Oh where is she? What's happening to her?

What if something's going wrong? Have I tried this place, that place?

Q Are you always thinking about her?

A It's like 24/7. You just can't get it out of your head. You're thinking, Where is she? What is she doing? Is she in trouble? Is she dead? Is she alive? It's just so horrible. It's the not knowing that's worse than anything.

Q What's it been like over the last two-and-a-half weeks for you?

A Horror. It's not even real. It's been really weird. Like why am I talking to a camera? Everything's just like not happening. Even my friends don't believe it. It's like a nightmare and I'm wondering when I'm going to wake up.

Q What's been the hardest thing for you to deal with?

A I think not knowing anything. We might as well be back to the second day she went missing. We haven't found out anything different. There haven't been any leads. No one's seen her. It's just horrible.

Q Is this the longest time you've spent apart from her?

A She's been away for five days and that's on a school trip. She's never been on a holiday with a friend or anything before. It's the longest we've not seen her without a phone call, email, text message or anything.

Q What's it been like for you at school? I know you went back this morning.

A It's been really hard for me. Everyone doesn't know what

to say to you. They don't know what to say. Some smile and some others think, Oh, God, what do I say? And others just wave. Hugs are hardest – all your emotions and everything.

Q What have people been saying to you?

A If there's anything they can do. But there's nothing anyone can do unless they can bring her back, which is what I really want. Everyone's been really helpful. They've been handing out leaflets and everything. We've had so many letters.

Q What has the attention been like?

A The media has been great. Everyone's been really friendly and helpful.

Q It's on your mind all the time. It can't be easy when you've got your GCSEs.

A It's really hard when you're trying to revise. You read something. I'm studying German and I end up thinking about Amanda. Like I could be learning how to say 'Let's go shopping' and then I'll just start thinking about her. Could she be shopping? There's just no point in me trying to revise because I can't.

Q What was it like over Easter for you?

A It was the first time we were going to have a big family bash at my uncle's house. It was going to be really good because Amanda was going to play her saxophone. And I was going to help making the dinner. We haven't seen our relatives from Devon for quite a while so it was all going to be really great, they were going to come up but that had to be cancelled obviously.

Q So when was the last time you saw her?

A It was in the morning before we went to school, in the car journey, she was really relaxed. Friendly. Normal. We got a lift to school together because Mum works there. We leave about twenty-to-eight. Amanda was cheerful, nothing was bothering her. She didn't tell me anything the night before. The night before that she'd been to a Pop Idol concert and was tired.

Q So she didn't seem upset? There was no argument?

A No, nothing. It was just normal. Put the radio on, had a good sing-song. I keep thinking what's the matter? Has something like a UFO taken her? It's really hard to work out what's happened to her.

Q What about the support?

A We've had loads. Tons of letters. People offering laptops, offering to take me to school. I found it hard to go out with my friends. When I saw my best friend, I cried.

Q What about the next day? Did you think she'd be there?

A It took me a while to realise that she'd actually gone missing. It was getting all serious. It took me ages to realise. It didn't sink in. In my mind it still hasn't. I don't know what to believe any more.

Q What do you want to say to Milly?

A There must be someone who knows something. Please call the police because we really need to know something. Even if something bad has happened, they've got to say so we can start to get over it. The grief. It's just awful.

Q What's it been like for you? You're her big sister.

A It's been awful. I would always look after her and she'd do the same for me. It's really hard because sometimes my mum starts crying and it sets us all off. My gran has been really good. I think she just blocks it out. She won't watch the news because it upsets her. It upsets me to see that home video because that might be the last time I see her or hear her again.

Q How do you cope with it at home?

A It's changed. Even if she came back now it'll never be the same again. I can't answer the phone now in case someone important calls. I try not to cry in front of them but it's really hard to stay strong.

Q When you see her on the TV and papers — how does that feel?

A Unreal. Why is this happening? What have we done wrong? A massive photo appeared in a paper and that was weird. That makes it hit home. How serious it is.

Q Have you had much support?

A I'd like to thank everyone who's been supporting us. They've been lovely. Ironing etc, fabulous. They've been putting up posters themselves.

Milly's godmother Sarah Ford also spoke of her torment in an interview organised by Surrey police. 'It is the not knowing that is the worst thing. Her parents and sister Gemma can't stop thinking about her, going over it in their heads, and they can't sleep or move on.' The 42-year-old, a teacher, said that, if Amanda had run away, the family could resolve the problem. 'I promise we can sort out whatever reason has made her run. If somebody is holding her against her will, they must release her and let someone know what has happened.'

Exactly one month after Milly disappeared, on 21 April, Hannah MacDonald shared pages from an intimate diary she kept with Milly – a 'friendship book' that not even their parents knew about. The world would eventually hear more of Milly's innermost feelings, those of a 13-year-old on the verge of becoming an adult, but this was an early glimpse at her thoughts. Hannah, a fellow Heathside pupil, said, 'Whenever we did something together we'd add a photograph and we wrote silly notes to make us laugh. This is my most treasured possession and it was Milly's too … Milly never said once that she was going to run away – and she wouldn't because she hates the dark. When she stays over, we keep a light on for her. And if she needs a drink, one of us goes downstairs with her. She's scared there might be a bogeyman under the bed.'

The girls' diary was kept in a yellow Winnie the Pooh ringbinder with the word 'Thoughts' on the front. The first page was decorated with a sketch of the pair drawn by Hannah's 16-

year-old sister, Louise. It was captioned: 'Hannah and Milly met in 1999 and here are a few photos they have taken throughout the time they've been matey-poos! Enjoy!!!' Hannah explained what it meant to them. 'We both loved the drawing my sister did.'

Among the photos are two taken by Sally Dowler in the previous May, when Hannah had gone to Selsey in West Sussex to camp with the Dowlers. Hannah said, 'When Milly saw my photo she laughed and said I was a poseur, so we had to write that in. Milly always writes the notes as she has the nicest handwriting.'

The final complete page of the diary contained the most recent photograph of the girls which was used on posters to highlight Milly's disappearance. 'We went into Woolworths in Kingston and queued for ages to get to the photo booth, but when I got to the front I realised Milly had gone. I found her tinkering with a *Thomas the Tank Engine* book that had a microphone to read the story through and a speaker. She decided to find out what happened if you held the microphone next to the speaker. The screech of feedback rang through the shop and everyone looked at us. Milly, totally straight-faced, said, '*Hannah!*' as though it was me. I went so red-faced and she was laughing. And then we had to go to the back of the queue again ... Until she comes home every empty page is a reminder that Milly is not with her friends and family, where she should be.'

Soon the number of calls received by police passed the 4,000 mark. Had she been abducted by a stranger? Taken by someone she knew? Had she gone off with somebody she met through the internet? Her friends and family insisted she could not have run away. The Dowlers made two tearful appeals for news of their daughter. Surrey police put on display a school uniform similar to Milly's and appealed for people to look out for a beige rucksack, a white purse and the Nokia phone. Hopes were raised only to be dashed after somebody rang to say they had found a white purse which turned out not to be Milly's.

Surrey police also responded to the criticism that detectives had failed Milly. The force said it 'committed significant resources to the investigation'. These included speaking to over 3,000 people, dealing with the thousands of telephone calls and searching more than 50 sites. Superintendent Sharp said, 'Throughout this investigation we have been painstakingly thorough, whether in terms of search activity, interviewing friends and family or house-to-house enquiries. We would urge caution regarding information given to the media from people not working on the case, as they are likely to be very misinformed. Ill-informed comments and speculation are obviously distressing to the family and is not helpful to the investigation. We are still treating Amanda as a missing person and will continue to do so until we have evidence to suggest otherwise. We are not treating this as a murder investigation but in resourcing terms we have more officers working on the Milly case than most forces would deploy on a murder investigation.'

Nevertheless, former Deputy Chief Constable of Manchester John Stalker wrote in one newspaper: 'The police search for Milly

Dowler has been confusing from the start. I have investigated hundreds of murders and inquiries like this need a strong sense of direction from day one. My feeling is that this one has lacked a sure touch from the beginning. It doesn't know whether it's local or national, a missing person or a murder, a uniformed or a detective inquiry. It has never been sure-footed … There have been many inconsistencies … We were also told there was no way Milly could have been abducted without being seen, but I saw plenty of quiet places on the road between the station and her home where a girl could be grabbed by one or two men in a car without witnesses.

'Walton-on-Thames is just three miles from the M25 and a car with Milly in it could have been hundreds of miles away before her worried parents called the police. The search should have been widened out to take that into account. It was more than a month before Milly's room at home was thoroughly searched – if it had been a murder inquiry it would have been done in the first 48 hours.

'I could not believe the police claim that they have not lost any forensic opportunities or other evidence by the delay. How would they know? The problem is that the police have tried to be sympathetic to the family, who have gone through a terribly tragic experience, at the expense of being hard-nosed and doing the routine things they have to. The search should now be reclassified as a murder investigation or a murder-style investigation to make it clearer to the public what is going on as this crime will only be solved with the public's help. I have daughters of my own and my heart goes out to the Dowlers. There are no right or wrong ways to hunt for Milly but at the moment this is manifestly an unsuccessful inquiry.'

There were also false alarms too. At one stage in late April, a female's body was hauled by police from the Thames near Milly's home. A police source said, 'It is obvious that it has been in the water for some time.' The body was carried to a blue-and-white tarpaulin tent which had been erected near where it had been spotted. 'A body was found downstream from Sunbury lock,' reported the police. 'We received a call from a member of the public who reported seeing something in the water.' It was not Milly. It was an elderly lady but even so tests had to be carried out before the news was relayed to the Dowler family.

Almost seven weeks into the hunt for Milly and with the *Sun* offering a reward of £100,000 to help find her, the family gave a brief interview. 'It is like a nightmare that never ends,' said Sally. 'It is difficult to sleep and when we wake up the nightmare just continues. Things that we used to think were important no longer are. The house is full of reminders, especially her saxophone and karaoke machine. It is particularly hard when we hear some of her favourite songs ... Someone out there must know something. It is like a living hell. If anyone has any information concerning her whereabouts, please find it in your heart to help us.'

Gemma said, 'My home used to be full of fun and laughter and now everything has changed. Milly and I were always singing, dancing and messing about and now we spend a lot of time crying and trying to make sense of it all.'

Bob said, 'Since Milly has disappeared, the feeling of everything in our lives changing has become immense. Little things will unexpectedly remind me of her and make me very sad.'

A 36-year-old man was arrested in Chertsey, Surrey, and a 52-year-old man in prison awaiting trial on alleged sex offences was also questioned, but neither was charged. At one stage, army experts – trained in finding buried bodies in the Bosnian war of the 1990s and its aftermath – were drafted in.

By 25 June, what would have been Milly's 14th birthday, police had already warned the Dowlers that is was probable that their daughter was already dead. 'Her birthday is going to be so hard for the whole family – for our friends and for her friends,' said the Dowlers in a statement. 'No one really knows what to do. For example, they're asking us if they should send cards. Any family occasions are really hard, even other people's birthdays. We go to send them a card, and then it hits us – who do we sign it from? Now we just put "the Dowlers". The whole concept of wishing someone a happy birthday is very hard to reconcile.'

Bob Dowler said, 'We usually celebrate Milly's birthday with something like a pool party. We have a 12-foot splash pool that we put up in the garden and have a barbecue with a dozen or so of her friends. She usually does something like that for her birthday. Maybe this year she'd have wanted a karaoke party. Milly really loves her karaoke. We'd probably have bought her karaoke tapes for her birthday. She loves all the usual teenage stuff. We were thinking we might have bought her a digital camera – she's always using the video camera.'

Sally said, 'I still send her text messages just in case and just wait for the failed message to come back … It would have been inconceivable if, when Milly first went missing, someone had said that we still wouldn't know what had happened to her by her birthday, especially given all the effort everyone has put in. We're so grateful for the efforts of the police and the support they've given us. We couldn't have asked for more. When we realise the extent of the things that they have done, we are staggered.'

The couple were quoted on how the family coped with Milly's absence. 'We're struggling to fill the days – we try to set ourselves a project but it's hard to remain motivated – we end up just going through the motions. But we have to try to hold it together for Gemma. She gets very upset when she sees us upset and wants us to keep positive and brave. It's frightening when we realise how many people are feeling this too. Lots of other people are hurting for us and not necessarily people that we know. We find that very touching. There are so many things that we miss – especially her playing her saxophone. The lack of noise is very noticeable – the house is so very, very quiet now.

'When Gemma has a friend round, we remember what it's like to have two in the house and how it should be. Because there are still posters up, we see her image everywhere we go. We know it's good to have so many posters all around but it's also very hard. We just can't believe that it's our daughter. We drive past and wonder, Will they still be here in six months? The [Queen's Golden] Jubilee weekend was hellishly long. Weekends are very difficult anyway. It was hard to see millions of people enjoying themselves. It would have been lovely to be one of them. Ordinarily, we would have done something as a family – like for the millennium, when we all went up to London for the fireworks. At one point, we had been talking with our neighbours about holding a street party.'

At around this time, several newspapers reported a change in the senior police officers handling the hunt for Milly. *The Times* said, 'The police officer leading the search for the missing schoolgirl Amanda Dowler has left the inquiry and returned to normal duties.' Surrey police said that Detective Chief Inspector Stuart Gibson, the divisional senior detective for north Surrey, left for work elsewhere. Detective Chief Inspector Brian Marjoram joined the team leading the investigation. He wasn't, said the police, 'a direct replacement for DCI Gibson'. Surrey police said that it was standard procedure for other forces to review the work of an investigation team, and in this case Sussex police had been asked to do so. The review had concluded that the inquiry was well run, but despite 'an immense amount of effort had failed to find the missing child or provide any evidence to positively indicate what might have happened to her'. Surrey police denied newspaper claims that a series of blunders could have hampered the search for Milly, *The Times* said.

In a last-ditch attempt to obtain information from the CCTV cameras on the Birds Eye building which should have picked up images of Milly if she had walked down the length of the road, police sent the video to the FBI's headquarters near Washington. The sun shining into the camera had made it difficult to spot specific objects because of the glare. Detective Chief Superintendent Craig Denholm was asked about the chances of the FBI cleaning up the film. 'We are hopeful but not optimistic,' he admitted.

The growing expense of the investigation was putting it under pressure and some officers were expected to be withdrawn unless a breakthrough came soon. DCS Denholm said it was highly unlikely that Milly had either committed suicide or run away, although both possibilities had been investigated. 'We have no body, no crime scene, no witnesses and no significant suspects,' he said. 'But with no crime scene, my officers cannot make forensic comparisons. It has been impossible to obtain a profile of the offender, because experts have nothing to work from. We reached five hypothetical explanations for Milly's disappearance. They were: abduction, self-harm, suicide, injury and running away.' Each has been eliminated, leaving only abduction. '

In August, two more girls made the headlines when they disappeared. Holly Wells and Jessica Chapman, both ten, vanished from the village of Soham in Cambridgeshire. Bob and Sally Dowler said in a statement, 'Our hearts go out to both sets of parents. As we watched the parents' appeal on television, we can say we know how they must feel and both felt overwhelmingly sorry for them. It's difficult to know what to say to them apart from to try and stay strong, which is extremely difficult. Obviously, we dearly hope that both girls are found alive and well.'

It was not to be. Holly and Jessica's bodies were found near RAF Lakenheath and school caretaker Ian Huntley was eventually convicted of their murder. And soon came the news that everyone had feared – Milly too was dead.

CHAPTER 3

It was almost six months to the day after Milly disappeared that the Dowlers spoke again of their torment. Even as they were doing so, by a terrible coincidence, the agony of not knowing what had become of their daughter was about to come to an end.

A married couple had found a skeleton in some secluded woods in the countryside. They did not report it to the police until the next day and then tests had to be carried out to see whether it was Milly. Simultaneously, the Dowlers were talking to the press, unaware of the significance of what was happening elsewhere.

Sally Dowler said, in an interview carried by many of the newspapers and other media, that she still treasured the video of Milly eagerly ironing her jeans in preparation for the Pop Idol concert. 'I just had to get the video camera and film her because it was the first time Milly had ever done any ironing. There was a

CD on and she was dancing away. Her sister was cooking tea in the kitchen which was unusual as well. As I videoed them they were taking the mickey out of me, saying I was sad. I used to think those jeans were ghastly. They're big, baggy things and frayed at the bottom. I'd think, Oh, if only she'd put something pretty on she'd look lovely. Now I pick them up and smell them – I smell her. I hug them and think, Oh, where is she?

'Just after Milly went missing, one of her friends brought round Gareth Gates's CD "Unchained Melody". There's a bit in it that says, "I'll be coming home. Wait for me." I just wept and wept when I played it. I still do – quite uncontrollably – if I hear that song. Sometimes crying helps. When I watch the ironing video I always think, That's Milly – particularly the silly little dance thing she does and the way she cocks her head at the end. It helps that it was taken so recently, just three days before she went missing. Milly was quite pleased with herself when we played the video back. She'd washed and done her hair and I think she thought she looked quite nice. Milly was not terribly confident. She'd need little pep talks and reassurance. You'd have to tell her she looked nice in something.

'In the beginning my brain went into overload and I honestly felt in complete fear of losing my mind. I couldn't cope because there was no answer. Right now, if you asked me, "What do you think happened?" I'd say she has been murdered. I haven't had that absolute feeling that it's happened at a precise minute. I haven't really gone beyond thinking, She's been abducted and she's dead.

What's happened in between is a gap. I can't bring myself to think about that bit. Until we find out for sure what's happened, it's too awful to contemplate.' The Dowlers had left Milly's room much as it was that third week in March with her teddy bear, CDs and saxophone in the usual places. 'It's the not knowing that's so difficult to cope with,' said Sally. 'When Holly and Jessica disappeared in Soham I felt so sorry for their mums.' But when their bodies were discovered the Dowlers said to one another, 'Horrible as the outcome is, at least they do know.'

'The other day I was chatting to someone I hadn't met before,' Sally said. 'She didn't know who I was and asked me how many children I had. I couldn't answer, I just cried.'

Sally had not returned to her teaching job and Bob Dowler too was on compassionate leave. He said, 'Nothing in your life can prepare you for this. Is it wrong to laugh and enjoy yourself? What I've said to people is, "You show me the rule book. You tell me what I should do now." I don't know if we're ever going to find out what's happened to Milly and it's the waiting for answers that almost drives you crazy. If someone does know anything or if they know anyone who's been acting suspiciously, please, please contact the police and help us.'

Gemma also spoke movingly of life without her little sister. 'A month after Milly went missing the police found a body in the River Thames and thought it was her. It just clicked for me that I was never going to see my sister alive again. But there was still a flame inside me that I might see her – a little flame of hope. Sometimes I think, Milly can do that with me. Maybe she'll be back by then. But then I think, No, I'm not going to see her again.

'Neither she nor I had ever been a bridesmaid and it was one of our lifelong ambitions to be each other's maid of honour. We used to go on the internet together to look at wedding dresses. It's really sad now. I can't be hers and she can't be mine. If I get upset, I play a CD and put the headphones on. It splits you up from the world and you can go into a little music world. The hardest thing is not knowing. The worst bit is seeing my parents so upset and not being able to do a thing about it. When someone dies you grieve but eventually life carries on again. When someone's missing you haven't got any of the answers. Mum will start crying and I don't know what to say to her. I can't click my fingers and bring Milly back and I can't say everything will be all right.

'[Milly and I would] chat about school and boys. We also used to send prank messages to some friends. We'd phone up and say, "Hello, this is the gas company. Is your refrigerator running?" If they said "Yes", we'd say, "Go catch it then!" and we thought it was the funniest thing in the world. Milly was really funny and very intelligent – more so than me, which could be quite annoying. She was with the in-crowd at school. She was cool. She wore the clothes and talked the talk. The only thing that ever scared her was the sea. Last Christmas we went to Cuba to swim with the dolphins. It makes me laugh when I look at that video now. She was really frightened of what was under the water even though it was as clear as anything. In that video she's clinging to me and Mum. Generally, she just took life as it came. Milly and I used to take the mickey out of Dad a lot. He'd come up with stupid phrases like, "Shall I log off now?" And we'd sit and laugh at him. Mum would laugh too. If he was telling us off for something, Mills would always say, "Mum, we know you want to laugh."

'The night before she disappeared she was talking about a Pop Idol concert she'd been to the night before. She said she really enjoyed it and had been singing her little heart out with her friends Hannah and Sophie. She said, "Night, night, Gemma, I love you." She'd say that every night before she went to sleep. She said it to Mum and Dad, too. She'd say it in case anything happened during the night so that she knew the last thing she'd said was, "I love you."'

A week before Milly disappeared, the girls had performed as the Beach Boys in a local talent competition. 'It's my favourite video of Mills and if I want a laugh I put it on,' Gemma said. 'We had surfboards and dressed in wetsuits as if we were going to the beach. We sang "Surfin' USA" and Mills looked so stupid. We did this stupid little dance and won an award. Sometimes, when I see my mum and dad so upset, I think, I could learn the saxophone, then I'd be able to take Milly's place,' said Gemma. 'But it wouldn't make anything better. It would probably upset them more.' From the first moment that Milly vanished, Gemma was convinced that she had been abducted. She would get furious with the police when they implied that Milly had run away from home.

'I used to get very angry with the situation. I couldn't understand why the police kept going down that route. I know she wouldn't have let Mum and Dad do those emotional appeals. Sometimes I have dreams that she's still in our life – that she's run away and come back.'

Gemma recalled the fateful afternoon of 21 March when, tired after having been on the trampoline, she lay on the sofa watching television. 'Mum came into the sitting room at about half-past four and asked where Milly was. I said she must be at a friend's house. Mum was babysitting for our nephews [actually cousins] that night and went out. Dad was working in the dining room. He came in about 5.00pm and said, "Gemma, where's Milly? She was supposed to be home at 4.15pm." He went out to check for her. I sent Milly a text message, telling her she'd better get home as Dad was really annoyed with her and would be very cross if she didn't get home soon. Dad drove all the way past the station to see if she was there but there was no sign of her. I was watching *Neighbours* so it must have been about 5.45pm when he came back in. He said he couldn't find her anywhere. Dad went out again and I started to get worried. I rang some of her friends, but no one had heard anything. That's when I thought she'd been abducted. I just had this really strong feeling that was what had happened. I was getting very frightened because I was in the house on my own. I thought, What if the man who has taken my sister is after me as well? What if he's after our family? When something like that happens you don't know what to think. Your mind races through thousands of different options and you think of the worst things.

'When Dad got back, I said, "We need to call Mum." Dad and I called all Milly's friends while we waited for Mum, but no one had seen her. When Mum arrived I said, "This is getting really serious now. We need to call the police." The police arrived shortly after 7.00pm and immediately treated Milly's disappearance as a major incident. Soon police dogs were searching nearby allotments and police helicopters flew overhead. I remember looking out of the window, thinking, Come on, Milly, come home. My mum kept going out to the front of the house, pacing up and down the street, looking for her at the end of the road. I kept thinking, This is a nightmare and I'm going to wake up soon. Then I would say to myself, Come on, wake up, it's beyond a joke now. I kept thinking, She's going to be with this friend or that friend. We'll phone her. And then she wasn't there. I was talking to our friends on the internet asking if anyone had seen her. A friend of mine said she had seen her walking along the road while she was waiting at the bus stop.

'Mum and I searched Milly's room for phone numbers of friends we didn't know. We'd see stuff that reminded us of her, and that was hard. Milly had this teddy that Mum had made for her. When you squeeze its tummy, it says, "Night, night, Milly. I love you." Mum got all upset when we came across that.

'We've got the same perfume. Mine ran out the other day so I popped in to Milly's bedroom and thought, I'm sure Milly wouldn't mind. Or if I'm going out I might say, Milly's not using that top, I'll just borrow it. I know Milly wouldn't want to see us all upset and worrying about her so I just think I'm going to enjoy myself twice as much – for me and Milly. It's like Milly is there too.'

Gemma was questioned by police officers for several hours in a suite specifically designed for talking to vulnerable persons, in Weybridge, Surrey, within a week of Milly's disappearance. 'There was lots of stuff they wanted to know – what we'd talked about the day before, what sort of stuff Mills used to tell me. They asked about boyfriends and what she did socially. It was quite hard because Milly had told me things in confidence. They asked me things about Mum and Dad. "Did they have an argument with Milly? Did they argue regularly?" I was in tears over certain questions and got quite annoyed. I said, "You shouldn't be asking me about my mum and dad. It isn't their fault she's gone missing. You should be asking other people." It felt like they were sucking all the energy out of me. Mum explained that the police might think Dad was a suspect or my uncles – all the males in our family would have to be questioned intensely. It was the worst feeling in the world to think that your dad was being questioned for something to do with your sister. I can't imagine what it was like for him. It was really horrible when he came back from the police station. And the police kept wanting more photos of Milly and taking away more of her stuff. They searched our whole house which was really horrible as it meant all her things had been touched. There was nothing left that Milly had been the last one to touch.'

Unable to sleep for three nights following the abduction, Gemma was prescribed sleeping tablets. 'When you try and go to sleep your heart goes, *boom, boom, boom*. And you think about everything. I had a panic attack and couldn't stop crying. Every time I shut my eyes I could see Milly being stabbed. It was the most horrible feeling. My mum and dad had to call the doctor and he gave me some tablets to calm me down. I also kept getting visions of her stuck in a room with this man trying it on with her and I couldn't do anything about it. I was supposed to be revising for my GCSEs, but I couldn't work. If I was doing German and there was a phrase like, "I'm going shopping", I'd think, Milly could be out shopping with the person who's taken her. In the end I got predictive grades that they took from my mock results and my coursework.'

Gemma added, 'I've got a boyfriend since Milly's gone. He keeps me happy. Milly never met him and that's upsetting because they'd have got on like a house on fire. In the beginning, you felt trapped. You weren't allowed to do happy things in case people judged you. We had to spend so much time together our relationships got very strained. Everyone changed so much. It was like something had taken over our whole family and everyone reacted differently to how they had before. You had to try to hold everything together. We had to stop ourselves worrying about stupid little things like what we wanted for dinner.

'We went on holiday in the summer. It was hard to go so far away. We felt we shouldn't be there. We went to a karaoke bar with a family who had two friends of Milly's and mine. Sometimes, if we sang a song, I'd think, This one is for Milly. And in my heart I was singing it for her. But I wouldn't say it out loud because it would have upset everyone. It was strange Milly not being there. She used to do little background bits and there was no one to sing those bits – so I kind of took her place in the song sometimes.

'I don't like to think about what's happened to her because it scares me. To think about what someone could have done to her makes me physically sick. Sometimes, if I go upstairs, I look out of the big window to see if she's there. I don't think my family will ever be the same again. It was my uncle's 40th birthday the other day, but Mum can't enjoy herself. You can't see her relax. Dad does sometimes, but you can't see him as his old self. It's much harder if you have an argument about something stupid like what time you have to go to bed. I feel really guilty. I think, Mum and Dad don't need this on top of everything else. Whoever's done this to Milly must have a family as well. Let's switch the situation. Would you like me to take your family from you? If I stole one of your family members, would you be able to feel how hurt we are? Anyone who suspects a member of their family should come forward.'

Irony of ironies, by the time those interviews appeared, the police hunt for Milly had ended. Over the six preceding months, a number of bodies had been discovered and checked to see if they were Milly. They had all proved negative – until now.

On Wednesday, 18 September, a middle-aged couple, Richard and Bogumila Wislocki, had been mushroom picking in Yateley Heath Woods alongside the B3013 Minley Road in Fleet, Hampshire. The tangle of birch, bracken and gorse amid the dark conifer trees made it ideal for mushrooms to grow in the wild. But the couple did not discover any mushrooms: instead, they found the skeleton remains of Milly.

Surrounded by barbed-wire fencing, the 250-hectare area was mixed woodland managed by the Forestry Commission and leased from the Elvetham estate. It was 25 miles from where Milly was last seen and, although it would usually take 35 minutes to drive there, the proximity of both the M3 and A30 roads meant it could be done in much less time by someone determined to drive faster. Lying three miles to the north of Fleet, the B3013 left the town's business parks to enter countryside with just five houses along the six-mile stretch of road which runs down the eastern side of the wood. The lane leading to where the remains were found was between Fleet to the south and three miles from Yateley to the north. The woods were not open to the public and few people would have known of the maze of paths between the conifers.

The next day, 19 September, the couple reported their findings to police and at 12.40pm spoke to officers on the Milly case based at Staines police station. Police accompanied the Wislockis from a gated layby into the wood. There was an earth mound, known as a bund, across the layby which was almost directly opposite Minley Farm, one of the few buildings in the area. A gap in the bund was wide enough for a vehicle to go through and, although there should have been a chain on the gate to the layby, fly-tippers were in the habit of breaking it to dump rubbish in the woods.

The police followed a track for about 75 yards before turning right and continuing for approximately another 75 yards into a wooded area. A skull and other bones could be seen alongside a small stream. Everyone withdrew and the area was cordoned off at 1.40pm. Scenes of crime officers arrived at 2.38pm to carry out a forensic search of the scene, recover the remains and to look for any other evidence. Samples were taken from nearby trees and other items in the hope that they might provide some DNA samples, fibres or perhaps even fingerprints. However, the scientists said that the chances of recovering any DNA were 'so low as to be unrealistic'.

Samples were taken of the soil and leaf litter in the hope that they would indicate how long the body had been there. The area in which the body was found was excavated at three levels and the material was removed for analysis. The soil was sieved. There was no evidence that there had been any attempt to bury or conceal the body. A total of 153 items of rubbish within the cordon were removed, many of them plastic ties the Forestry Commission use to fix signs to trees and posts.

On 20 September, consultant pathologist Dr Hugh White and colleague Dr Jonathan Musgrave visited the site of the discovery. There was no clothing nearby nor were there any of Milly's possessions. The bones had been scattered by wild animals. The remains were taken to North Hampshire hospital in Basingstoke where a post-mortem was carried out. It was impossible to say how the victim had died but 'she had been dead for months, not weeks', Dr White was to say. Dental records and DNA samples were to identify the remains as Milly. Dr White deduced from the absence of insect activity around the remains that there had been no injuries to the soft tissue of the body, no cuts and no lesions. The indications were that she was dead when she was left there all those months ago.

Detective Superintendent Alan Betts of Hampshire police said, 'This afternoon dental comparisons were carried out at the North Hampshire hospital in Basingstoke by a forensic odontologist. She compared the remains in Yateley Heath Woods found yesterday with the dental records of Amanda Dowler. We can now confirm that the results of this examination that the remains are almost certainly those of missing Amanda. Our thoughts and sympathies are with Amanda's family at this very difficult time.'

Local farmer Peter Page said, 'The police turned up yesterday and didn't tell us a thing. We had to watch the news to find out why they were here. It's horrible to think this is where Milly's body was left. The area is always busy with dog walkers from all over.'

Another farmer, Frederick Stoddart, said, 'It's terrible to think something like this could happen so close to your home. My thoughts are with Milly's family.'

Glyn Willoughby, Heathside headteacher, said, 'We are all very distressed by Amanda's tragic death and extend our sympathy to her family. We are also thinking of Amanda's friends who will be very upset by this terrible news. When it is appropriate, we'll think about what we can do so Amanda will always be remembered here.'

Murder hunt head Detective Chief Superintendent Craig Denholm said, 'The news that we have found what we believe to be Amanda's body is very distressing to everyone involved in this inquiry and much more distressing for Milly's parents and her sister. Our worst fears have been confirmed. But we are now much closer to discovering what happened to Amanda. We know which direction we are heading in. No stone will be left unturned in the hunt for the killer.' Detectives believed the murderer was a man with local knowledge of the site of the kidnap and the ground where the body was dumped. They were to be proved right in both respects.

The 10am service at the 850-year-old St Mary's parish church in Walton-on-Thames that Sunday was a heart-breaking affair. Bob and Sally walked arm-in-arm to the church and Craig Denholm was there to comfort them. The couple wept quietly along with many of the congregation throughout the holy communion service. The Rev Graham Holdaway led the service and spoke of how the police had to face recovering Milly's remains and it was too much for Sally. Her cries of anguish rang out, forcing many in the congregation to cling to each other for support. Gemma had decided she was not strong enough to attend but the sisters' grandmother was there.

Mr Holdaway, who had taught Milly maths at Heathfield, lit a candle for her soul. He said, 'Last March we lit a candle in hope that Milly would return to the love of her family and friends. That hope has been taken from us but we light a candle with a different hope. We shall remember her. We will give thanks for her life, we will recall any memories we have of her and I will recall a lively, cheeky, talented pupil.' He prayed for all those involved in the investigation 'and particularly those who have had gruesome tasks to fulfil over the last few days. We support them with our prayers as they search for justice for Milly. We find it hard to forgive the deed that has brought us so much grief. Milly is free from the past and all its hurt and rests for ever in the calm security of your love.'

Several youngsters held their heads in their hands and many stayed on their knees through the 45-minute service, unable to stop the tears flowing. Emotional parishioners in the packed congregation clutched bunched-up hankies as they listened to the Rev Mary Stokes give the sermon. She spoke of the unjustness of life and the 'sheer force of human evil' which had robbed the Dowlers of a daughter.

Floral tributes were laid throughout the community – at Milly's school, at Walton-on-Thames railway station, at the end of her road and along the route from where she was assumed to have been snatched. A large colourful poster, attached to a tree on Station Avenue, read, 'We will never forget you and your smile. You will always be in our hearts.' Milly's close friend Cara Dawson had left a poignant card beside it saying, 'I will miss singing "Angel" with you every Friday night ... lots. I will miss the sound of your laughter and I wish I could have just one hug from you.'

There was also a growing pile of bouquets at the entrance to Yateley Heath Woods and a photograph of *Pop Idol* star Gareth Gates was among the flowers.

Six sniffer dogs on loan from the Metropolitan police were brought to the woods to hunt for the rest of Milly's remains as more than a hundred police widened their fingertip search to a 600-acre area. Officers handed out fliers at a market at Blackbush airport on the nearby A30 appealing for help to trace the youngster's clothes and possessions, including her grey-and-navy school uniform, Nokia mobile and white ace-of-hearts purse. More than 6,000 motorists were stopped in the area around the woodland in the following weeks.

The Dowlers issued a statement: 'At last the long, agonising wait is over. Now we can bring her home and say goodbye – a feeling of relief but so very, very sad. No one can hurt her now, our darling Milly. However, we will not rest until the monster responsible for this ghastly crime is brought to justice and behind bars.'

On the Monday, schoolmates gathered round the mass of flowers and tributes at the school entrance and many brought bouquets and personal messages. One read: 'Now you are in heaven, the angels and fairies will look after you.' Another said: 'You are a very special friend and always will be. Love Hayley.' There was a collage of pictures of Milly with the message: 'Lots of love, miss you, Mel and Kirsty'.

The youngsters had been prepared for the worst since hearing on Friday that the remains found in the woods were almost certainly Milly's. That day had already been set aside as one of remembrance for the teenager because it was six months since she had gone missing. The results of tests on the body had come through at 5.00pm after the children had gone home for the weekend. On Monday, local education officer John Ambrose said, 'The nice thing is that they did support each other and they were also supporting the staff. In a way, it was good that they had gone home when the news was confirmed because they were with their families. We were still talking about what to do at 8.30 this morning before students arrived. But I think today is about reacting to their needs – we are being led by them. At the school there are educational psychologists on hand for any pupils who need support. We have also talked to parents over the last six months, mainly those of students in Milly's year group. Heathside is a very close community and this just made everybody even closer. It is terribly sad but the students support each other.'

Elsewhere, a small roadside chapel in Milly's memory was set up, close to the spot where her body was found. A book of condolence was opened in a portable building set up at the scene and turned into a unique shrine at Yateley Heath. It was blessed by a curate, vicar Robin Ewbank from the nearby St John's Church at Hartley Wintney, who placed candles there. The vicar said, 'Around 30 people have signed it already. They have mostly been local parishioners but some have been up to lay flowers by the forest. A lot of people are grieving. We have lit some candles and put some nice flowers at the back of the church and we are open for people to come and pray.'

Eight days after the discovery of Milly's remains, Sally and Bob Dowler made a poignant journey to Yateley Heath. Sally placed a single white rose on a grass verge close to where Milly's body had been found and Bob put his arm around her as they struggled to hold back the tears. They had been collected by police from their home in an unmarked silver people carrier and taken to Hampshire. Forensic officers in white suits carried on with their work as uniformed officers guarded the site. The couple spent several minutes in the hut looking at the scores of bouquets and reading a book of condolence and their inscription simply read 'Bob, Sally & Gemma'.

They then returned to the car and were driven along a tree-lined path into the forest accompanied by Detective Chief Superintendent Denholm. An eyewitness said, 'It was a very highly charged and emotional visit … A barrier kept them away from the areas which have still to be forensically examined but they were able to see for themselves the spot where Milly's attacker finally dumped her body. Mr and Mrs Dowler remained composed throughout the whole visit and had the benefit of police family liaison officers with them.'

On 8 October, a memorial service, simply called 'Remembering Milly', was held at Guildford Cathedral as her parents launched a trust to prevent 'another tragedy' at the hands of child killers. The congregation of 1,200 was given an order of service with a picture of Milly's smiling face on the front and celebrated her life, as Bob said, 'Milly seemed to have touched so many people in her life, many we know and some we may never know. We are so grateful that Milly was able to pack so much into 13 happy, healthy years and bring us so much happiness.'

He added, 'She was many things to many people – a loving daughter, a sister, a granddaughter, a niece, a cousin, a best friend and a pupil.' His wife, he said, would miss hearing her say 'lovely mummy' and he would miss searching for the CDs of his she borrowed to play and they would all miss her untidy bedroom and her jokes at their expense. Her grieving father also talked of their pride at her achievements, and especially her saxophone playing. The hour-long service included two performances by her school's saxophone group, including the Carly Simon song 'Nobody Does it Better', which Milly had played as a solo shortly before her disappearance.

Bob Dowler comforted Lindsay Dobson, a family friend who had known Milly since she was born. Lindsay broke down as she delivered her tribute. She recalled how her family had once sat with the Dowlers and talked about what their daughters would become when they grew up. 'When it came to Milly we thought maybe a vet, a presenter or even an entrepreneur. This evil deed has taken away my opportunity to watch Milly grow but I have seen enough to know we were shooting too low. Milly would have made a real mark on this world – a real difference.' She recalled Milly's fondness for 'those terrible baggy jeans that she wore'. She said that many people had seen the pictures of Milly ironing her jeans. 'Milly ironing! That wasn't the girl I remembered.'

The ironing was unusual but that brief video did, however, reveal the real Milly, said Mrs Dobson. 'The smile on her face that comes from her eyes, her constant need to be dancing or moving as she sways with the ironing. Her inherent "coolness". Actually, it is the girl I knew – and the girl we will all miss dreadfully.'

Hannah MacDonald read out a poem she had written. It was 'to my friend' she said. It included a verse which read: 'When I go to sleep at night, you join me in my dreams. Life is how it used to be, happy, loud and full of fun. Oh, if this were only real.'

Milly's uncle, Peter Wood, sang 'You'll Never Walk Alone' and Glyn Willoughby read from I Corinthians. Denis O'Connor, the Chief Constable of Surrey and DCS Denholm were also in the congregation.

In his address, Right Rev Ian Brackley, Bishop of Dorking, said the purpose of the service was to remember Milly with love and affection and to express heartfelt grief. 'So much goodness, goodwill, and human warmth and compassion have emerged out of all this to restore some faith in our human nature and life together,' he said. 'For it would be a victory for those forces of darkness that infest the minds of thankfully a tiny majority of the human race that wishes to harm, abuse or exploit our children, if we over-reacted now by becoming too protective of our young people and over-suspicious of one another.' He praised the Dowler family for establishing Milly's Fund, a charity aimed at helping children and young people to become more aware of personal safety. At the end of the service, Gemma released 25 balloons outside the cathedral doors. They were carried away by the wind and Bob and Sally then comforted their elder daughter as she was overcome with tears.

In early November, there were hopes that a breakthrough had come in the hunt for the killer when the model of car spotted on CCTV footage from the Birds Eye factory was identified as a Mazda MX-6. Surrey police had asked FBI experts to compare images of different models of cars from the footage and the sporty coupe was seen driving slowly down Station Avenue about 4.15pm. The driver appeared to stop and talk to a pedestrian who police believed may have been Milly. Despite numerous appeals the driver of the vehicle had never come forward so police were tracking down the owners of every model in the Surrey, Hampshire and London areas. DCS Denholm said police still needed to talk to the driver of the MX-6 caught on camera. 'They may have information that is vital to the investigation. I would appeal for anyone who is the owner of such a car and was in the Walton area about 4.00pm on Thursday, 21 March to consider whether it may have been them and to contact us.'

When the owner did come forward, it transpired that she, her son and his fiancée had stopped in Station Avenue to make a telephone call from the kiosk there as they were lost and they had called an estate agent for directions to a property they wished to see. The hope that the person talking to the Mazda driver might be Milly proved fruitless: the blurry image they had of a pedestrian talking to a car driver was simply the son having a conversation with his mother.

As Christmas drew close, Sally Dowler made a public announcement about Milly's Fund. 'Long before they found Milly's body I was sure she was dead,' she said, 'but I knew there was no point wasting all my energy imagining the horrible scenarios of how she might have died because that would just be too upsetting. Then, when her body was found, it opened another chapter because at last you allow your mind to think the unthinkable. I also began to wonder what sort of person could do this to my beautiful daughter. I still can't get my head round that. I have learned to take each day as it comes. I have good days and bad days but now I know there's nothing I can do about what's happened. All I can do is try to prevent it ever happening again … People started phoning to ask where they could make a donation.

I was very keen on doing something concerning personal safety for young adults.'

Sally Dowler added, in the lengthy interview in the *Sunday Express*, 'When Milly first went missing, I was often asked whether she was the sort of girl who might get into a car with a stranger. At first I said, "Definitely not" – after all, she was sensible and not at all gullible. But then you examine every possible scenario in your mind and I realised it was too easy to say definitely not. These people have ways and means … The situation with Milly was extreme – she disappeared coming home from school on a busy road in the middle of the afternoon on a bright, sunny day. However, I don't want to frighten anyone or make children feel scared to go out. I want them to feel confident and happy like Milly did because teenagers should be having the time of their lives.

'Right from the start on the day it happened I knew something was wrong. She had rung to say she would be half an hour late, but then an hour became two and we rang the police. Not knowing was the worst thing of all. At first I went into shock. I remember thinking to myself, You have got to pull yourself together for Gemma's sake. I also remember saying to my husband, Bob, "I've got enough for me and enough for Gemma but for the moment I can't cope with anything beyond that." So, for a long time, we dealt with the trauma alone. Nowadays, however, what tends to happen is that if I'm having a bad day Bob will be the stronger one and vice versa. If you have had a really strong relationship, you can't go through something like this without it making you closer. Normal life just disappears …

'When they confirmed it was Milly's body, it was a huge relief. I thought, Thank God they've found her – now no one can hurt her, we can bring her home and say goodbye properly … Reality always hits. Last week we went to the woods where her remains were found. We had been to the edge of the area before but this time we went to the actual spot. Gemma came with us and it was absolutely heart-wrenching. It's very difficult for her because she misses her sister so much. She desperately wants to laugh again and I tell her it's so important that we all laugh. For her sake I try not to sit around being depressed all the time …

'I have been overwhelmed by the enormous public response. Opening the post is always challenging, because you never know what you are going to get. I have received hundreds of letters. There have been some incredibly moving letters which take great strength to read. Unfortunately, we have also had our fair share of cranks. There was even one sick woman who rang pretending she was Milly.'

On the first anniversary of Milly's disappearance, 21 March 2003, the girl's funeral took place. Unlike the memorial service some months before, this was a private affair, although for ten minutes the traffic was halted near Walton station as the Dowlers led a group of about 20 mourners in a procession along the road. A cortege of a hearse and four cars pulled up opposite the station.

The hearse carried her coffin and a display of flowers arranged to spell her name. The centrepiece of the many tributes was a huge floral saxophone, with a bumper box of Maltesers tucked in underneath – two of Milly's favourite things. Police motorcycle riders stopped traffic and a single rider, in black, went ahead of the cortege as Bob, Sally and Gemma led the group as they walked slowly behind the hearse.

Behind them was DCS Denholm, with two family liaison officers. A small bunch of white flowers was placed, above head height, in a tree close to the spot where the teenager was last seen. Another bunch of flowers lay on the steps of the station entrance, with a message: 'Dear Milly, I cannot believe a whole year has gone by. You have been missed terribly by everyone. We all hope that you can now rest in peace for ever.'

The funeral took place at St John's crematorium in Woking and afterwards the Rev Margaret Callow said, 'We held a simple service, at which Bob and Sally made their personal tributes to Milly and a piece of music called "For Milly" was played, which had been written and recorded by her saxophone teacher.'

The Dowlers released a statement: 'The 12-month anniversary of Milly's last day with us is a very poignant occasion for us and we feel that it is right to mark it by finally laying her to rest. We will not be able to rest ourselves until we see whoever is responsible for murdering our daughter brought to justice. Milly was a beautiful daughter and our lives have a huge gap in them without her. We all miss her spirit and laughter terribly.

But we are trying to carry on as best we can, especially for Gemma's sake.'

Later in the year, a 70-strong children's choir performed a specially written piece called 'Milly's Song' at London's Sadler's Wells, with the proceeds going to Milly's Fund. In total, some 500 youngsters aged 5 to 18 from theatre schools around the country appeared at the concert. 'Milly was in the school orchestra and the saxophone group. It was something very dear to her,' explained Sally. 'When Milly was at home she was always making up little dance routines with her friends and her sister Gemma. She also adored singing and loved karaoke. Milly's friends from her music group at Heathside School are taking part in the show and that is something very special for us. Many of Milly's friends and family will be in the audience. It is a wonderful way to remember her. And to have the event in somewhere such as the Sadler's Wells Theatre is very special.'

Bob Dowler said, 'Music and dance were a big part of Milly's life. Many people will remember the film we released of her playing the saxophone. It means a huge amount to us that the public haven't forgotten Milly and that this evening is being dedicated to her … They approached us in February and we immediately thought it would be a fitting memorial for Milly … There is nothing we can do to change what happened to Milly but we decided to try to prevent such a horrible thing happening to someone else's child.'

Yet, just one month earlier, in February, when the Dowlers had already been approached about the concert and were also, no doubt, making the arrangements for the funeral service, another family were about to experience the agony that they felt. Levi Bellfield was to strike again.

CHAPTER 4

Marsha McDonnell was killed by Levi Bellfield as she made her way home, just as Milly Dowler had been 11 months earlier. Tragically, Marsha had almost arrived at her front door, and she was just yards from safety when he struck.

Gap-year student Marsha was just 19. She lived in Priory Road, Hampton, near London. Hers was a long, quiet road with solid Victorian houses at one end which gradually gave way to more modern buildings that nevertheless still exuded comfort and security.

The evening had begun for Marsha with a trip to the cinema. She and two friends from work were dropped off at Kingston Bridge in Kingston town centre at 8.30pm. They were near the White Hart pub, just over the river from Marsha's workplace, the Wax Lyrical candle shop in the Bentalls shopping centre.

Much later on, at 12.07am on Tuesday, 4 February 2003, Marsha boarded the 111 bus from Kingston. She paid her fare with 70p from her purse and moved to the back of the bus on the lower deck. At 12.17am, she was the only passenger to leave at her stop on Percy Road and she started on the 500-yard walk home. Nearby was a silver Vauxhall Corsa, a five-door hatchback, behind the wheel of which was Levi Bellfield. The bus CCTV captured the car's movements as Bellfield drove past when it stopped to let Marsha off. The Corsa itself halted in the mouth of a junction and was then lost by the CCTV camera as the bus pulled away.

Bellfield was tracking the bus, waiting for a victim. He had a hatred for all women, especially blondes, and Marsha, like Milly before her, was in the wrong place at the wrong time. Her body was found on the pavement in Priory Road. There had been three separate blows to her head causing severe brain injury. There were no 'defence injuries' which indicated that she had not even had the chance to protect herself. He had approached from behind and struck.

Marsha's mother Ute was still waiting up for her when the girl's body was found by a neighbour on the pavement at 12.30am. She was taken to Kingston hospital and diagnosed as suffering multiple skull fractures and massive bleeding around her brain.

After conducting house-to-house enquiries in the streets and roads surrounding her home, police said nothing had been stolen. Her bag was recovered and her mobile phone was still in her pocket. It obviously was not a hit-and-run and Detective Chief

Inspector Christopher Watts, leading the investigation into her death, said 'There was no outward sign of struggle.'

The attack took place about five miles from where Milly had disappeared and a Metropolitan police spokesman said the force would work closely with Surrey police. 'All lines of enquiry will be pursued,' he said.

The McDonnells had lived in the area for over ten years. Her father, Phil, was a former music tour manager for Van Morrison, Fleetwood Mac and Clannad, who had then started a freight company specialising in the entertainment industry. He said, 'The pain of Marsha's death is simply indescribable and I know it will never go away until the day I die. Already it is like a huge, ten-kilo weight hanging on me. Already I'm thinking of the birthdays and Christmases ahead when Marsha won't be with us.'

Her mother Ute said, 'She packed so much into those 19 years and thank God that she did, but it is terrible to think that her life was ended with such terrible violence. What kind of person could do this to someone who had so much love for other people?'

Mrs McDonnell had last spoken to her daughter on that Tuesday evening. With just one more day to work before the closure of the candle shop, Marsha had gone out for dinner, followed by that trip to the cinema. She was hoping that she would travel to Australia later in her gap year, helped by money she was saving. 'The last thing she said was, "Do me a favour", and she asked me to tape a programme for her elder sister. She had forgotten and felt bad about it. She was very sweet that way. She always wanted to do things for people.' Her mother often worried about her making that journey, even though it was barely 500 yards from the bus stop to the house. 'I always hated her taking that late bus,' she said. 'It was such a walk from the bus stop and you just never know what kind of horrible people might be around.'

A neighbour living opposite the local greengrocer had been woken by a loud thud and found the teenager suffering from terrible head injuries. At 1am, Mrs McDonnell heard a ring on the doorbell. 'I thought it was Marsha and assumed she had left her keys again, but it was a policeman at the door. My stomach just went. They asked me for a photograph and to describe what she was wearing.'

Mr McDonnell drove to the hospital. 'As I drove past the police cordon I could see the whole pavement covered with this huge pool of blood,' he said. 'I was looking at this in horror and asked the policeman if it was from my daughter. He said, "I am afraid so."' Following x-rays and brain scans on Marsha, doctors told the family that she would not recover from her injuries. 'The doctor and the nurse came in to see me with their heads hung low. I knew it had to be bad and I said, "Cut to the chase. Is it life-threatening?" And they told me it was.'

One of Marsha's sisters, 14-year-old Maya, was able to be at her bedside while the other, 21-year-old Nathalie, was away the USA. The family kept the tragedy from their five-year-old son Jack. Her father said, 'Although it was such a terrible time, the atmosphere was absolutely fantastic. We were all around her and we hugged her and held her and told her how much she was loved. She could not have been surrounded by more love when she died. When they took away her life support, it took a while for her heart to stop.' She died at 4.30pm on the same day she had been admitted to the hospital.

Mr McDonnell revealed Marsha loved mixing and had joined him at pop outings where she met stars like Oasis drummer Alan White. Phil said, 'She lived life to the full. She would go out with her friends night after night and be absolutely wrecked. I would say, "For God's sake, have a night in, catch up with your sleep." She'd go upstairs then one of her friends would ring and instantly she would come alive again, leap into the shower and be off out again. That was the kind of person she was.'

Mrs McDonnell said, 'She was so full of life, she was a real toughie. I had to leave her for a short while to come home and put Jack to bed. I told her to hang in there for me until I got back and she did. She loved life and when she left us in that hospital room she was surrounded by love. We all said goodbye to her and when she went it was with great love.'

Her heartbroken mother revealed the family had almost lost Marsha to meningitis when she was just four months old. Originally diagnosed with ear ache, by the time she finally reached hospital she was fighting for life. Ute said, 'They told me she was so ill that if she lived she would be deaf and dumb for life – but she went on to be a brilliant violinist. I felt afterwards I have been very lucky – but I have not been lucky twice.'

Mrs McDonnell remembered the day their dog Daisy, chosen by Marsha at Battersea Dogs Home, died aged 15 and was being buried in the garden when Marsha said, 'Wait.' 'She rushed inside for a gold medal she had won at netball that meant so much to her and put it in the grave with Daisy. It was very moving – but we all laughed later at the thought of someone discovering the bones in the future and being so puzzled that there was gold there as well.'

Marsha had studied photography, psychology and communications at college and her mother said, '[She was] tremendous at netball. She was the rock all her friends depended on and now she has gone. I had four children before and if anyone asks me in future how many children I have I will tell them I still have four because for me Marsha is always going to be here. We had hoped that at least when Marsha died they would have been able to use her organs to help others – she would have wanted that but they had been too badly affected ... This is so terrible for us – but for Jack I think it will be worst. They were very special to each other, complete soul mates.'

And as forensic experts continued to scour the scene of the horror, Marsha's friends paid tribute to her. Ashley Clifford, Jo Gutridge and Hannah Cash had known Marsha for years and they had joined old schoolmates – and Marsha's then boyfriend Jake Smith – for a holiday in Newquay, Cornwall, in 2001. Ashley said, 'Marsha was gorgeous and funny – she was always happy and always crazy. She was friends with everyone and never stopped taking the mick out of herself. Marsha loved having a good time but she was always there for everyone. If anyone was upset they would want to talk to her – she was a shoulder to cry on.' Ashley recalled a scene two years earlier in a local park: 'It is one of my happiest memories. We were doing an art project together at school. We took pictures of each other laughing and paddling in the water.'

The last time the two had seen each other was in the candle shop a week before Marsha's death. 'Marsha was one of those girls everyone loved as soon as they met her. I split up from my boyfriend about the same time she split up from Jake. She really cheered me up, telling me I deserved better and making me laugh. Jake was her first serious boyfriend, her first love, and when they split she was really upset. But she always made an effort to seem all right on the outside even when she wasn't. When I last saw her a week ago she looked amazing. She'd had her hair and nails done and was wearing lovely new clothes. She seemed really excited and really happy again. She was always starting trends – she was the first person at school to wear high heels and I thought she was so cool. She even had buffalo boots like the Spice Girls.'

Another friend, Laura Scott, said, 'She was always dyeing her hair – ginger, blonde, brown, black, you name it. Once we dyed our hair red. I did Marsha's and she ended up with a red scalp. She was really bubbly and making jokes and doing crazy things.'

Hannah and Jo were too upset to talk of their loss but their parents said how badly it had affected them. Staff and pupils at

Marsha's old school, Waldegrave in Twickenham, were also coming to terms with the tragedy. As well as being a talented violinist, Marsha had captained the successful netball team. Headteacher Heather Flint said, 'She had so much potential. Everyone here is shocked.'

A week after the attack, Nathalie McDonnell, a student in her third year studying for an advertising degree, described her sister as a 'free spirit' and said the days since the murder had been 'a massive nightmare'. 'Even the night she died she telephoned my mum to tell her to tape the Michael Jackson documentary for me. She always thought of other people.' Nathalie broke down in tears as she described her feelings. 'I can't take it in. It's just like it's not real. You wake up and wonder if it actually happened. It's just a nightmare. Every time something like this happens and you see it, everyone always says it's a nightmare. But it really is just one massive nightmare, every time there's something that reminds you of her, the things she used to do and places she used to go, people she used to hang out with, every little thing.'

Detective Chief Inspector Richard Freeman appealed for four people to come forward as they might have vital information about the moments leading up to Marsha's murder, which they now believed to have been 'an unprovoked stranger attack'. How true that phrase turned out to be. He said that they had identified almost all of the bus passengers on the 111 apart from two men who appeared to board the bus together outside the John Lewis store. Two more people, who travelled on the 70 bus late on

Monday 3 February between Kingston and Hampton, were being sought as potential witnesses. 'This is an extremely difficult investigation. Most murders do carry a motive with them and many have witnesses. Anyone who knows anything, however large or inconsequential they think it might be, do not hesitate to call us. Everything will be dealt with in confidence wherever we can.'

Three weeks after Marsha's murder, a BBC *Crimewatch* reconstruction of the attack took place. Police hoped that the reconstruction would provide vital evidence to identify the attacker who was thought to have also assaulted two other young people with a hammer or heavy piece of metal in the area. Hundreds of viewers responded to the programme, police said. Detective Superintendent Alastair Jeffrey, who appeared on *Crimewatch*, said, 'We have had an overwhelming response, it has been excellent. We heard from a number of people who may have been in the proximity at the time. Obviously, we need to get in touch with them and see if they can take the investigation any further. We have had a large number of people naming individuals who they have a particular concern over. That has come from the medical profession and also friends and relatives. It is a real concern with some people and we will prioritise these cases. We believe a local man could be responsible for these attacks. He is probably a young man, but it is difficult to say what age.'

Police reinforcements were drafted in to Hampton to carry out stop and search operations on cars and pedestrians as well as increasing night patrols. Superintendent Sue Hill, in charge of policing operations in Richmond, said, 'We would ask everyone in the area, please help us catch this man. Someone must know who is doing this. A young girl has lost her life and this is everyone's problem.' She advised people to take common-sense precautions when they were walking in the area late at night, especially to be alert and aware of their surroundings.

The sixth-form college in Richmond, where Marsha had studied, urged students to take 'extreme care' when out at night. It warned, 'Students will be aware of the terrible tragedy of Marsha McDonnell's recent death in Hampton and you will also possibly be aware that a 17-year-old girl suffered injuries in Strawberry Hill in January. The college has received unwelcome information today that one of our male students was attacked in the early hours of Tuesday morning in Hampton, although fortunately without serious injury. In the circumstances the college urges all students to exercise extreme care with regard to the potential danger associated with being out late at night, particularly unaccompanied.'

On 7 March, more than 500 friends and family gathered for Marsha's funeral at St Francis de Sales Catholic Church in Hampton. The coffin, decorated with cherubs, was carried by four pallbearers. Phil and Ute McDonnell walked either side of her little brother, Jack, and they were followed by Nathalie and Maya, hand in hand.

Irish group Clannad, the band Mr McDonnell had worked for as a tour manager, played from a balcony and the Van Morrison classic 'Brown Eyed Girl' was chosen for the coffin's exit. Marsha's uncle, Mike Hywel-Davies, read a poem. In place of flowers, the family requested donations to the Shooting Star charity, which was building a hospice for terminally ill children close to the family home. The service was conducted by Father Bernard Boylan, parish priest of Hampton, who told the congregation Marsha herself had made monthly contributions to a children's charity. 'It was given in the proper Christian manner, with no other member of the family knowing anything about it until after her death when these things come to light,' Father Boylan said.

He also spoke of the crime that 'so hurts and scandalises our very humanity', asking 'What is our life about that can be subject to such wanton and brutal destruction? What is human freedom for that can be summarily and viciously cancelled without cause or reason?' He spoke of Marsha's 'enthusiasm, her gift for friendship, her readiness for adventure and her inner happiness'. Father Boylan said that Marsha epitomised the joy of youth with her love of sport, music, art and her gift for friendship.

Another uncle, Shane McDonnell, said, 'We now have the chance to allow Marsha to rest in peace for ever. We want to gather and celebrate the beautiful life she had and remember all the joy and happiness that Marsha brought us.'

Six months on from the murder, police were still hunting for Marsha's killer. A Met spokesman said, 'At this stage, no one is charged with the murder of Marsha McDonnell. We must stress, however, that until such time as someone is charged our enquiries remain very active. Our advice to members of the public, particularly vulnerable people or lone women, is to continue to take sensible precautions.'

Ute McDonnell's words at that time have a chilling resemblance to those uttered by the parents of Levi Bellfield's many victims: 'We miss Marsha so badly. The person who did this to her has no idea what he did to her family and friends. He might as well have put a dagger into all our hearts. I'm not sure you can ever really deal with it, it's just about coping with the grief. As a mother, it's like part of you dying. You have carried them in your womb for nine months and loved them. You have all these hopes and dreams for them and you do everything you can to keep them safe. How can you bear it when something like this happens? It is your worst nightmare, the kind of thing you see in television programmes and just pray will never happen to you. It all felt terribly unreal, that this ordinary suburban scene could suddenly have turned into such horror.'

She also spoke of the effect the loss of their daughter had on her husband and other members of the family in her interview with the *Daily Mail*. 'He has found it very, very hard to adapt. He did do some work from home when he could but it was only a couple of months ago that he felt able to go back to the workplace. His grief is like a wound with just a very thin layer covering the top – you only need to brush against it and it's still so raw. It was different for me, in a way. I had to keep some kind of normality going. To take our son Jack to school, I had to walk past the spot where Marsha was killed, four times a day, then deal with the parents at the school gates, so I was in at the deep end from the start. In a way, that was better. I thought, I can either put the hammer to my own head, or I have to cope. Marsha was such a family-loving girl that I know she would have wanted us to carry on and make the best of it. I just had to deal with it, but Philip didn't have that. He hid himself away.'

Nathalie gained a 2:1 degree at university, although she had wanted to delay her exams for a year. 'I have to tell her Marsha would have been thrilled for her. Maya, who's 14, is finding it very hard. She coped very well at the beginning but now the grieving process has kicked in. She's at a difficult age as it is and coping with the reality of bereavement was always going to be hard.' Of Jack, she said, 'I think he is only really now understanding that she isn't coming back and what death really means. How could we convey that to a little boy? All we can do is give him security and love. I feel desperately sorry for her friends. At their age a death is so difficult to cope with. They used to think they were immortal. I really feel their pain.

'What I would like is to see the person who did this put away safely and securely so he can never do it to anybody else. God forbid that anyone else should ever have to go through what we have over the last few months. We have to remember that Marsha would have wanted us to carry on as a family, to remember her with a smile. So that is what we have to focus on when the going gets tough, not on anger or hatred. It's hard, but the consolation I have is that her 19 years of life were filled with love and laughter. A lot of people are never fortunate enough to experience that in their whole lives, so I can be grateful for that. And when her friends talk about how they remember her, they say it is with a smile. That's a wonderful legacy.'

One year on from the murder, Ute talked of the family's charity work, saying they would continue to support Shooting Star with the fund set up to pay for a music therapy room in the Hampton Hill facility. 'As we approach the first anniversary of Marsha's death, the family wish to focus on the positive through the Shooting Star Hospice for children. This is what Marsha would want. We still support the work of the charity and always will for Marsha's sake. I would urge people to continue donating to the fund in her memory.'

Marsha's elder sister Nathalie was later also to talk of the impact the murder had on their family. 'As children, we always looked out for each other and, although Marsha was two years younger than me, she was our protector. When I was five and someone stole my bucket at a playground, it was three-year-old Marsha who got it back for me. As young adults, Marsha and I became more like friends than sisters … At the start of February 2003, I was looking forward to a week in New York as part of my graphics course. The evening before I left, we had a family dinner. Marsha came home from the candle shop with presents for everyone from the shop as it was closing down. That night, Marsha and I watched television and chatted. Eventually I went to my room to pack. "I'm coming to check your case and make sure you haven't taken any of my clothes," she joked. I didn't kiss her or hug her goodbye because I was only going for a week, so it wasn't a big deal. "Do you want me to get you anything?" I asked. "Bring me back a cool T-shirt," she said. These were the last words my sister ever spoke to me.'

In New York, Nathalie returned to her hotel at night to find Laura, an old family friend who lived in New York, waiting in the lobby, along with the college secretary from her university. 'I could tell from the look on her face there was something wrong. "Nathalie, I have something to tell you," she said. "There's been an accident." My first thought was that something had happened to Mum and Dad. "It's Marsha," Laura continued. "She's in hospital." For Laura to be there, I knew it must be serious. She thought Marsha had been mugged but didn't have any details. My parents had left a garbled message on her answering machine.

'My uncle and cousin were at the airport to pick me up. I was expecting them to take me straight to Kingston hospital to see Marsha but instead we headed home. Alarm bells started ringing. My brother Jack ran to answer when I knocked on the front door. I'm sure he thought it would be Marsha. I walked into the living room. Dad came straight over and gave me a hug. "I'm so sorry, Nat," he said. "Marsha died at four o'clock this afternoon when you were on the plane."

'Deep down, I think I already knew. I felt numb. I sat down on the sofa next to Mum and Maya and wept. I could see Dad crumbling before my eyes. Jack was sitting on the floor drawing –

Mum and Dad had explained Marsha was dead, but he was too young to understand … The next morning, my first thought was, Is this really happening? When I went downstairs, the house was full of police officers and there were journalists camped outside. Later that morning, the police asked if I knew of anyone who had a motive to murder my sister. "Marsha didn't have an enemy in the world," I told them.

'A couple of days later, I decided to go to the spot where Marsha had been attacked to place a flower. My stomach churned when I saw the police murder board appealing for information. I prayed she never knew what happened. Just over a week after Marsha's death, the police asked me to stage an appeal to help catch her killer. Tears streamed down my face as I told a roomful of journalists about the nightmare our family had been trapped in since Marsha's death. The police quickly came to the conclusion the attack had been totally random. CCTV pictures of her on the bus home were published in the press. I knew it was essential but my grief was unbearable. She looked so happy and relaxed – yet a few minutes later she was dead. Marsha's death is enough to cope with. I can't imagine how I'll feel if there is ever a trial … Everything is "before Marsha" or "after Marsha" and that is the way it will always be.'

CHAPTER 5

evi Bellfield liked buses and bus stops. They were ideal hunting ground for him. There would be young women leaving the vehicle and they would often be alone and vulnerable. They would invariably have a solitary walk home in the dark along the streets of south-west London that he knew so well. He knew where to look and, importantly, he knew the escape route he could take. That's what he really liked: he could strike and then vanish into the darkness from where he had emerged. They literally would not know what had hit them. That is what had happened to Marsha McDonnell, attacked from the rear with no chance to defend herself.

His next victim was 18-year-old Kate Sheedy. This attack took on a different form and thankfully and miraculously she survived. His would-be murder weapon wasn't a hammer or heavy implement – this time he wanted to kill using a car.

It was just after midnight on Friday, 28 May 2004 and Kate was returning home from a night out in Twickenham at the Sorting Room and the Hobgoblin pubs. She was celebrating school leavers' day at Gumley House Convent School in Isleworth where she had been head girl. Kate was going to prepare for her A levels. She got off the 22 bus at a stop in Worton Road, Isleworth and began walking home. She became suspicious of a people carrier in front of her. It was a Toyota Previa and, although parked, the engine was still running.

Feeling threatened, Kate moved to the other side of the road but, as she crossed the mouth of a turning leading to an industrial estate, Bellfield struck. The lights came on, the engine revved and the carrier drove off – only to turn at speed. After performing a U-turn, it drove directly at her. She saw that the driver was hunched over the steering wheel – this was the position Bellfield often adopted, rocking backwards and forwards as he drove. He aimed the vehicle at her.

Kate tried to run for safety but there was no time and the vehicle hit her. Then, almost unbelievably, it drove over her again as she lay in the road. Young Kate suffered massive injuries. It was astonishing that she was not killed outright. Her lungs had been so badly damaged that she could not call out – she could barely whisper. Incredibly, badly injured as she was, she managed to reach her mobile phone and call home. She told her mother, 'I'm dying.'

Eileen Sheedy, a primary-school teacher, quickly called an ambulance then rushed out to find her daughter. 'Kate had managed to pick herself up and stagger a short distance in an attempt to get home. But she collapsed due to the horrific injuries inflicted on her,' she would later recall. Before lapsing into a coma, the teenager would tell police she was hit by a 'light-coloured' vehicle. The police began to investigate the possibility that the hit-and-run was a deliberate act by someone she knew but, unsurprisingly, officers were unable to find anyone with a grievance against her.

At West Middlesex hospital, doctors found Kate had a collapsed lung, a fracture of the clavicle and serious injuries to the abdomen and the liver. Her injuries were life-threatening and she was transferred to King's College hospital where she was placed in the liver intensive care unit until 14 June. She had further surgery to her liver and also to her back. Her discharge from hospital came on 21 June, although she had to be readmitted in September for follow-up surgery.

Headteacher at Gumley House Convent, Sister Brenda Wallace, said, 'We are absolutely shocked at what happened. We have prayed for her all day. Kate's a lovely girl who plays as hard as she works. She plays the flute in church and we fully expected her to get three As in her exams. She's a strong girl with lots of character and she'll be able to dig deep.' That's exactly what she did and, almost four months after the attack, she was able to recall the events of that evening, not knowing, of course, the nature of the man behind the wheel that night.

'The day had gone so well. I did the welcome speech and it was such a nice day, everyone enjoyed it but it was emotional too. As much as we were ready to leave, it's still the end of an era and we're leaving our friends after seven years.' After getting off the bus, she had started out on the short journey home. 'There was a white people-carrier after the junction with Farnell Road and it had its engine running but the lights turned off. Initially, I thought it might be a taxi dropping someone off but it struck me as odd because it had blacked-out windows. I just got a really bad feeling about it and didn't want to walk past it so I tried to do the right thing and crossed the road. But as I crossed the entrance to the industrial estate the van turned its lights on, U-turned and came straight for me. I tried to run but they hit me and I fell on my front. Then they reversed over me. I was just thinking, Why are they doing this? It didn't feel real. It was unbelievable and went in slow motion. I was frozen with the shock of it. When it happened for the second time, I felt completely crushed but I didn't notice that my back had been ripped open.'

Her mother explained what happened next. 'I went outside and couldn't see anything, Kate had been so calm on the phone that it made me wonder if it was a dream so I went back to check her bed.' It was only when Kate called for a second time that her mother managed to locate her. 'I didn't expect to find her in the state she was in, as she was conscious and calm. That was the most shocking thing. It felt like ages waiting for the ambulance to come. I think it was only about ten minutes but it seemed like forever and we couldn't understand what was taking it so long.'

Kate's father, who also lived nearby, arrived on the scene and the three of them went in the ambulance to hospital. Kate described what happened: 'They gave me a head and neck brace and I was vaguely aware that my dad was holding something up to my back. When they put me on my back that was the first time I felt in absolute agony and I was begging them to put me back on the pavement.' Kate was unable to recall much of the ambulance ride apart from becoming annoyed that she could not remember the names of the doctors and nurses who attended to her and that she refused to let them cut off the jewellery she had recently been given for her 18th birthday. 'It's quite difficult to imagine being so close to dying. No one likes to think that they nearly died but I was on a ventilator for a while as I couldn't survive my injuries breathing by myself as my lungs were so damaged.'

By August, she told her local newspaper, she had not slept properly for a long time and she did not like being alone in the house or going out alone. 'Even when I'm out with others, I'm always looking around. You always think something will happen to you when you're far away from home travelling or something – but it didn't and it shows it can happen anywhere.' Kate, who initially felt there may have been two people in the vehicle, added, 'There doesn't seem to be any reason for the attack, nothing we can think of or know of. If there was a reason, it might make it easier, but it's worse to cope with as I'm always questioning why they did it and where they are now. I feel sick that they got away with it and it feels like it never happened, apart from my injuries, as no one has come forward and no one seems to have seen anything. It's unbelievable.'

'There must be someone out there who knows something or who saw the van on the night. They are out there, but everything I do there is a reminder of this incident. I can't go to uni, I get tired all the time. I can't even go out on my own. My whole life has been affected by this at the moment. It's so unfair that this happened.' She was hoping to go to York University to read history and politics, her entry having been delayed for a year because of her injuries. Yet, sadly, even as she talked in mid-August 2004 of her ordeal, another young woman was to become Bellfield's next victim – and she would not survive.

Of all the settings for Bellfield's savagery, none could provide a greater contrast to the evil he perpetrated than the site of Amelie Delagrange's death. On the night of 19 August 2004, the 22-year-old was murdered by Bellfield on the cricket pitch at Twickenham Green, a triangular piece of greenery alongside a busy main road where, legend has it, WG Grace once played. The pitch, on the surviving fragment of the eastern section of Hounslow Heath, was home to Twickenham Cricket Club, who were proud to say they could trace their lineage back to 1833. A year after Amelie's death,

Prince Edward opened the new pavilion, just a few yards from where she died.

Surrounding the pitch were a row of Victorian cottages, a Congregational church, a Baptist church and the Archdeacon Cambridge Church of England Primary School. Salvation Army bands played there until modern times and maypoles would be erected on May Day. Arthur's on the Green restaurant was on one tip of the triangle. And to complete this idyllic setting, a Fuller's pub, the Prince Bulcher, proudly stood guard at the eastern end of the pitch. It was a perfect setting for ordinary people to enjoy the pleasures of the English way of life: cricket, pubs, churches – it couldn't be more delightful. For Levi Bellfield, it was perfect too, a perfect place to kill.

Amelie, like Kate, had spent the night in Twickenham with friends, in this case at a wine bar, the Crystalz. She took a 267 bus home at 9.45pm and five minutes later got off, having missed her stop. She walked back up Hampton Road to get to Twickenham Green which she crossed to reach her home. French-born Amelie, who spoke fluent Spanish, had arrived in London on 15 May to try to improve her English and had planned to stay until Christmas. She already spoke the language, having lived in Manchester in 2001 as part of her studies, and now she rented a room in a Victorian terraced cottage. It was one of many in the area, just a ten-minute walk from Twickenham Green.

Passers-by saw her consulting a bus timetable and then she walked along the eastern side of Hampton Road towards a pedestrian crossing near the cricket pavilion. Cameras on a route 70 bus captured her image at 10.01pm, the last time she was seen alive. As she crossed the Green, she was attacked and struck over the head with a blunt instrument. Like Marsha McDonnell before her, she could not defend herself and she too suffered massive head injuries caused by an attack from behind.

PC George Roberts was flagged down in his patrol car by a member of the public. 'I remember immediately seeing that she was in a very bad condition. There was a large pool of blood surrounding her head. She didn't appear conscious and I knew that she was breathing because it was almost like she was snoring.' The policeman said a female colleague tried to speak to her without success. He went with her to West Middlesex hospital in an ambulance and was with her when she was declared dead shortly after midnight.

Bellfield had sat in a white Ford Courier van and waited for his victim to walk across the Green. On this occasion, he took her possessions with him, including her Sony Ericsson T300 mobile and a light-brown handbag.

Her parents, Dominique and Jean-Francois, came from a tiny village 60 miles north of Paris. Days later, they visited the site where their daughter died and prayed on bended knee for several minutes, accompanied by Amelie's sister and uncle. Mrs Delagrange – who plucked a handful of grass – left a handwritten note: 'Amelie, my angel, why do you leave your mother? I keep you in my heart forever and I keep your smile.' The family laid a bouquet of lilies for the girl they nicknamed Lilibelle. Her father led his family across the grass. His message read: 'You will always stay alive and stay in my heart, my little darling Lily. You, whom I found so beautiful. Daddy who always loved you.'

There were 20 other messages on floral tributes at the spot and the parents paused to read them. Cristelle Peart, a 26-year-old language teacher, had laid flowers and said, 'I use the park whenever I can. On my days off I like to sit on the grass and read a book in the sunshine. You feel safe here, even in the evenings, because, wherever you stand, the road is visible on every side. It's unlit at night but if you're familiar with the area it doesn't seem dangerous. There's a path that runs right across the middle and I've never felt threatened when I've walked across it. Perhaps now I should.'

Amelie worked at a patisserie, Maison Blanc, in nearby Richmond where colleagues remembered a popular, happy girl who 'enjoyed every single thing about London'. The manageress Teresa Rubina said she saw Amelie about four hours before she died when she came to give her her new mobile-phone number. 'She was happy and smiley as always.'

Back in France, there was horror at the young woman's death. The killing was big news in her homeland, the newspaper *Le Parisien* devoting almost an entire page to it under the headline: 'SCOTLAND YARD ON THE TRAIL OF THE MURDERER'. *Le Journal du Dimanche* asked, 'Was Amelie a victim of the hammer killer?'

Delagrange had grown up in Hanvoile, a village in the rural

area of Oise. The family's neighbour was the mayor, Thierry Maugez, who said that she was a 'very nice child, very smiley, very pleasant and very polite. We are shocked and disgusted by what has happened. It is frightful and horrible. I only hope now that they catch the killer.'

Amelie's murder brought back shocking memories too to Ute McDonnell. 'When I first saw the picture of Amelie, I thought, Oh, my God – that's Marsha. They looked so alive, both young, blonde and very pretty. They were happy girls who only wanted to get on with their lives. We are now back to square one. This is like a flashback. The big question is why? Why would anybody take somebody's life like this for no reason?' Her heart went out to Amelie's family. 'It's so, so bad that they have to go through what we have been through for the last 18 months. The loss of their beloved daughter. She was so like Marsha in that she was such a lovely and beautiful girl.'

On 24 August, some of Amelie's belongings were found dumped in the Thames: a set of house keys, a purse and a Sony CD walkman were fished from the water by police frogmen beneath a bridge at Walton. It was five miles from the attack but just one from the spot where Milly Dowler disappeared. Specialist police divers hunted for her phone, her handbag and the rest of its contents.

The first suggestion that Milly and Amelie might have been killed by the same attacker began to appear but police, publicly at least, were not confirming it. However, attacks on other women in the area had caused a wave of concern. Police increased night-time patrols and installed extra CCTV cameras. Detective Chief Superintendent Andy Murphy warned women to be vigilant, avoid dark areas and cross the road if they thought they were being followed. 'We have to put things into perspective,' he said. 'Attacks like this are very rare.'

Rare they might be, but there was growing speculation that there was a link, somewhere, and that one man might be behind some, or all, of the recent spate of attacks. It emerged that a woman called Dawn Brunton, 36, had been assaulted from behind and possibly with a sledgehammer, near Heathrow in west London. Police confirmed they had questioned Ms Brunton, an accounts clerk, about possible links with the murder of Amelie. Ms Brunton, who was another blonde, was attacked as she walked down an alleyway towards Hatton Cross underground station. She suffered multiple injuries in the November 2003 attack.

She said, 'When I heard about Amelia's murder I was in absolute shock, there are so many similarities between what happened to me. My attacker came from behind and the last thing I heard was the rustling of leaves before he hit me on the back of the head. I fell down unconscious without putting out my hands and landed on the left side of my face smashing my bones and teeth. I remember thinking about taking the bus along Hatton Road and went to the bus stop but became impatient and decided to walk. I never expected something like this to happen to me. Nothing was stolen. I can't imagine what type of person would attack women with a hammer. When I think of what happened to Amelia, I'm lucky to be alive. My life was probably saved because I was discovered quite quickly by passers-by who raised the alarm and called an ambulance. I had five, big oozing lacerations, swollen lips and bruising and the back of my head had been fractured as had my cheekbone,' she said. She eventually needed three operations to reconstruct her face. Her recovery took seven months and she had titanium plates inserted into the back of her head and in the left side of her face.

DCS Murphy said, 'We have spoken to Ms Brunton and are reviewing evidence relating to the assault to establish if there is any link between that incident and the murder or any other attacks that have taken place in the area.'

Police investigations included an attack back in January 2003, in which a blonde 17-year-old female student was beaten over the head and left for dead in nearby Strawberry Hill. Then Edel Harbison, who was 34, was attacked near Twickenham Green in April 2004. The attack left City accountant Edel traumatised: 'I wish to express my deepest sympathy with the parents and family of Amelie Delagrange. It has been four months since I was attacked and this incident has brought back to me how fortunate I was to survive. Although I am still suffering as a result of my injuries, I was getting to the stage where I could start to think and talk about everyday activities and not the assault. This has been and continues to be a very distressing time for both my family and myself. But I am determined to assist the police in any way possible to catch the person or persons responsible.'

A week after Amelie's murder, a young policewoman retraced her last steps as part of a reconstruction aimed at tracking down her attacker. CCTV footage of her bus journey had already been released and now PC Sarah Swift, 5ft 3in and a size 12 like Amelie, retraced the French girl's last steps. Police hoped to jog the memories of people who may have seen Amelie shortly before her death on her route home. The officer, dressed in identical clothes – white zip-up cardigan, red top, white cropped trousers, white backless trainers – followed in Amelie's footsteps from the wine bar where she drank with four friends to the spot she died.

Amelie's close friend Teresa Rubina also visited the murder site. The pair had worked together at the cake shop in Richmond and Amelie had popped in on the night of her death to give Teresa her new mobile number. Later, Teresa had to identify her body. She said, 'It's like we lost a part of us when she left.'

Amelie's parents returned to the scene and they had a statement read out by a French-speaking police officer: 'Amelie, after being in Manchester in June 2001 in the course of her studies, was keen to return to England to improve her English. In April 2004, after a short period with the help of a French friend (who was herself established in London), she managed to find a place to live and work in a pleasant part of London. Amelie very soon made a strong circle of friends with whom she worked and socialised. The warmth of friends and the English way of life compensated for her family not being with her and because of that she envisaged staying longer in England. Her radiance and joy of living, described by her friends, was brutally ended at 22 by the mad actions of a predator. The news that we have heard has brought us indescribable pain which has devastated our family. In our time of grieving, during our stay in London, the efficiency, service and quality of the support from the Metropolitan police which has been offered to us have kept us strong during this time to find the person responsible for this terrible act. During the emptiness that we feel when thinking of our daughter and sister who was killed in abominable circumstances, we urge everyone in and around the local area to help the police with their enquiries and give evidence. Thank you.'

Throughout the story of Levi Bellfield, there is a recurring theme: the little tricks of fate which placed his innocent victims in his path. Amelie was the same as the others: in her case, a missed bus stop was crucial. Yet perhaps he would have found her anyway, no one will ever know. A French boyfriend, Olivier Lenfant, 25, talked of how he had turned down the chance to be with her just two hours before she was found dying. He said, 'Amelie rang and asked me to come over and stay that night and the whole weekend. She said her landlord was away and it would be just us. It would be lovely. I said I was really, really tired, too tired to come that night, but that I would love to come for the weekend. I promised I would see her the next day. She said she was going to go home for a quiet night, too. That was at 8.24pm. If I had agreed to meet her, she might not have even gone to a wine bar to meet her friends … not have been taking the bus … walking home alone. All our friends say I cannot blame myself. But maybe …'

That was the last time he spoke to Amelie. Her grieving parents, he said, 'wanted to know everything about Amelie's life in London, how she found happiness here and what it was about this place that she thought was so special. It is as if they wanted to fill in all the months when they did not have her with them and to understand the new life, so different from theirs, that she liked so much in Britain. Her mother has a smile just like Amelie's and she is a very strong and very sweet woman. But seeing them was very sad. You see, it was her mother who had encouraged Amelie to come and improve her English in London, saying it would be good for her.'

He explained how the pair had met at the Maison Blanc where his friends worked. 'I didn't talk to her much that first time, she was making chocolate boxes. But I think I had a small crush on her right from then. She was so lovely, always smiling and laughing. She was a very kind and giving person. Later, I saw her at a party and we kissed. It was very special but neither of us wanted it to happen. She had just stopped seeing someone else and I was in an unhappy relationship. We said, "Let's forget about it." But over the weeks the attraction became irresistible. At first, we had to have a sort of hidden, secret relationship. It was just the weekend before Amelie died that we finally spent the night together at our friend's place, Teresa, who runs the patisserie. It was like a small celebration … food, drinks. It was just so wonderful to be happy and be together.'

Olivier was woken in the early hours of the night of the murder when police phoned the flat he was sharing with a French friend. Officers had found the number on a scrap of paper in Amelie's pocket and at 4am they arrived to ask who knew a girl who might have that number. 'They said she had been attacked. They described her and I realised they were describing Amelie even though the police didn't have her name because her bag was missing. Then, early in the next morning, I was told she had died in the hospital.

'It is hard to believe she is really gone. I have not seen her body, her other friends went to identify her. Her parents returned to France on Friday but I think they still believe their little girl is in some way still alive in London. I don't think any of Amelie's friends will be able to accept her death until the killer is caught and she is buried, at home, near to her family. I still keep waking up in the morning expecting my phone to ring and for it to be Amelie.'

Another friend of hers also spoke of that night when Amelie died. Geoffray Vast was one of those out drinking with her less than an hour before she was battered to death. He said, 'We're all scared and trying to be more careful. Nobody goes home alone now, no matter how short the distance.' Amelie had gone off early because she was working in a delicatessen the following day.

Geoffray and the other friends later watched police cars flash past – unaware they were racing to the scene of her murder. Geoffray said, 'I'll definitely move now. Staying is a constant reminder we aren't safe. I pass the Green at least ten times a week and it's full of flowers in memory of her. I'd rather remember her angel face smiling at something stupid I've said.

'The police came to my flat. At first I thought it had to be a joke, but I realised it had to be something really bad. We are all really upset, we just can't understand why. Why Amelie? Why did it happen?'

Hundreds of people attended a memorial service on Twickenham Green on a Sunday soon after her death. Around 300 people paid their respects in a service led by the vicar of the Holy Trinity Church, the Rev Mike Starkey. Prayers were also said by leaders of many local churches during the service. Reverend Starkey said, 'There was a good cross-section of the community. This has obviously touched a nerve with local people and they appreciated the chance to come together and acknowledge what had happened and say prayers for her and her family.'

In mid-September, Amelie's funeral was held in the vast, old abbey of St Germer-de-Fly in Oise, France. Even though it was the largest church in the area, it could hardly contain the 700 mourners who came to remember her life. Relatives, old school friends, teachers and intimates from London packed into the 11th-century building, many of them having to stand at the back or at the side of the building. On the front of the order of service was a picture of Amelie, dressed in a white blouse and summer skirt, dark glasses on her head. Each of the members of her family spoke at the service: her sister Virginie gave a reading and her mother Dominique read a poem by Victor Hugo, her voice so cracked with emotion she could hardly get the words out. Her cousins even wrote a song for her which they sang at the end of the service: 'Sing, so we can forget our sorrow. Sing, so we can say we love you. But whatever happens, always sing.'

Her father said, 'Amelie, you left this world without saying goodbye to your family and friends, a sudden and brutal departure caused by an act of madness which leaves a huge void where you used to be … For us – your parents – your gaiety, your jokes, your humour, your daily presence, your beauty – spiritual as well as physical – your love: we will miss it all, always. But it is a comfort to us to know that your last hours were gay, full of feelings of love and lived to the full. This is not an *adieu*, it is not even *au revoir*. In our hearts you have not really gone: unseen, you will be with us always.'

Two of her friends, Morgane and Aurélie, also spoke about the girl they called Lili. 'You were always smiling, always there for us. You lived life to the full. The only thing that brings us any comfort today is the fact that we knew you.'

Also at the funeral was Detective Chief Inspector Colin Sutton, the officer leading the murder investigation who, as we will hear, was to play a key role in the hunt and eventual capture of Bellfield. He was accompanied by two colleagues from

Scotland Yard. 'I am still hopeful we will catch the killer. We have got lots of CCTV. I think we have got the killer on film. Now it is just a matter of finding out which one he is among all the people … I have got six men working round the clock. It is so moving and so sad that a young girl should come to our country and end up like that. You can see from the number of people here that it has moved the local people and we share their sadness today.'

By the third week in September, a special squad of experienced detectives at Scotland Yard had been formed to investigate the assaults. Each victim was a woman who had been attacked from behind with a blunt weapon while walking alone. The attacks took place in a five-mile radius that, paradoxically, had always been considered one of the safer areas of London.

'We are now formally linking a number of attacks,' a spokesman said, confirming what many had been thinking for months. 'The investigation has not revealed any forensic links for the incidents or anything linking the victims. However, there are some similarities in the profiles of the victims that are being linked. There are also similarities in the times, the nature of the venues and the mode of attack.'

DCS Murphy said, 'It is entirely possible that we have got more than one attacker out there. We have linked the attacks for the purposes of investigation.' Tellingly, he added, 'It's more about what we can't prove than what we can prove – we are unable to show that these offences were not committed by the same person.' Four suspects had recently been arrested in the Richmond area and released on bail. 'The fact that they have been arrested doesn't mean that any of them are the prime suspect. Somebody has committed some terrible offences. There may be in the days leading up to the attacks or in the immediate aftermath, a change in them. They may become sensitive or reclusive. On the other hand, there are certain individuals who are able to commit terrible murders and go about their everyday life. There are very cool operators. Our advice is for people to be aware of their surroundings particularly when walking late at night, coming home from the pub or work, when you may tend to switch off. We would just ask people to put it in context, ask women to take stock of what they do and how many times do they go out on their own and nothing happens.'

Speaking in the wake of the official announcement that police were sure there was a connection between the attacks, Marsha's mother Ute said she had always felt there was a link. 'The pain continues and all we can do is hope and pray this monster is caught – it is the horrible waiting game. He is a coward who waits in bushes for a vulnerable target and attacks from behind. What warning can you give when there's someone like that about? If a cowardly man is determined to attack women, the only way to prevent more attacks is for him to be taken off the streets. We had suspected for so long that the two murders [Marsha and Amelie] were linked. Geographically, it was obvious. The cowardly brutality made it even clearer. We've spoken to police before about the possible connection.'

Two months after she was murdered, a moving tribute to Amelie took place in Twickenham. Over a hundred mourners set off from a gallery by the river on a gloomy afternoon and made their way to the town centre along the riverside where Amelie often walked with her friends. Many clutched flowers as they walked and passers-by stopped to pay their respects as the sad procession, organised by friends from Maison Blanc, made its way through the centre of Twickenham. They walked to the Green where a sapling horse chestnut tree was planted to commemorate her life.

Dominique Delagrange later said, 'There is always the thought of Amelie's absence that never leaves us. In all honesty, we don't really live our lives any more, we simply survive. We think all the time about the *joie de vivre* that Amelie had and how much she gave to our lives. People talk about getting over loss, about grieving through the pain threshold. But in all honesty, I don't know what that means. To us, her death will always remain unacceptable. Her bedroom has remained just like it was before she departed, when she lived here. We haven't touched anything. We are a very close family. We miss her enormously. There is a huge hole in our lives. I don't think we will ever be able to bring ourselves back to normality, to go back to the way things were before. We are broken.'

Her architect husband said, 'There are horrible events

everywhere in the world. Things like this happen in France too. We don't have a bad impression of England because of what happened. Amelie was happy in her life there and met lots of good friends. Although it is hard, we want to go back to that tree every year to think of Amelie. It is at the exact place where she was killed and brings us closer to her.'

Survivor Kate Sheedy was also to reflect on the impact the attacker's madness had on her. 'My life was completely ripped apart on that night in May,' she said. 'Even now I'm still recovering from both the physical injuries and the psychological trauma I suffered … I have a 25-centimetre scar on my back and I also have scarring on my legs. The scar and the pain and discomfort I still feel in my back are a constant reminder of what happened to me. I don't think I'll ever be able to leave all this behind. I was unable to sit my A-levels and therefore unable to start university when I intended. It was very hard to say goodbye to my friends when they went to university as I felt like I'd been left behind. I can't wait to finally start next September. It has been extremely difficult to recover from this incident. I am still having counselling and trying to regain my physical fitness through physiotherapy sessions. I have only recently been confident enough to leave the house alone but still won't stay by myself after dark. I also suffer from panic attacks, which are very unpleasant. This incident has had a profound effect on my friends and family, who have all been a great support to me. It is incomprehensible to think that someone would try to take another person's life in such a cruel and callous manner. To target innocent young women is cowardly and sickening.'

The hunt for the man who was bringing terror to London was now dominating the headlines, and in early October Sir John Stevens, the head of the Met police, was reported as saying, 'We will catch this person as sure as night follows day. The resources are currently in place to solve the murder and I want to reassure residents will remain there until the killer is caught.'

And that was exactly what happened.

On Monday, 22 November 2004 came the news that everyone living in fear in the monster's hunting ground had been waiting for. It was on the radio, television and in newspapers not only in the UK but also throughout the world. The fear created by the 'hammer killer' had merited coverage from Australia to America and throughout Europe – especially, of course, in France. It was a major news item when police got their man.

Agence France Press, the wire service for France, reported: 'British police on Monday arrested a 36-year-old man on suspicion of murdering a French student in August, Scotland Yard said. Amelie Delagrange, 22, was murdered in the west London neighbourhood of Twickenham Green as she returned home on 19 August from a night out with friends.' Scotland Yard's Commander Andy Baker described the man as a 'suspect' rather than the less formal 'person of interest'. He said there were 'reasonable' grounds for the man's arrest. Other sources said the arrest was 'a significant development'.

As well as being arrested in connection with Amelie's death, the man was also arrested over the previously unreported attempted murder and robbery of a woman in 2002 near Twickenham Green. The victim, who was not born in Britain, had only come forward after the murder of Amelie. Many other girls and young women were to be named before the end of the saga as possible victims of the man now in custody behind bars.

Soon he was named: wheel clamper and nightclub bouncer Levi Bellfield.

CHAPTER 6

Levi Bellfield, the big, bullying beast of a man who liked to terrify women, was naked and hiding in the loft under a roll of roof insulation when his reign of terror came to an end. He lived with his girlfriend Emma Mills and their three children in a small, modern home in West Drayton. Their road was a small cul-de-sac called Little Benty near the M4 shortly before its junction with the M25. The area was a 1960s hinterland near Heathrow, full of traffic islands, confusing road signs and airport hotels: boy racer driving territory.

Emma had met Bellfield in the mid-1990s when he was a doorman at Rocky's nightclub in Cobham. She later recalled the arrest: 'It must have been four or five in the morning when they came. The house was lit up with torch lights and I thought he must be in trouble with the police – he'd been in trouble before, for fraud. But this was different. There were about 30 policemen with guns, there were dogs – all surrounding the house. They were banging on the door and screaming his name. I thought, What the hell have you done now? We were in bed and he turned and he just looked at me and he looked so scared. It was complete fear. I've never seen him look like that before. He said, "I'm sorry," and then he ran out on to the landing, pulled out a chest of drawers and used it to jump up into the loft. That's the last time I ever saw him. I went downstairs just as the door flew open and a load of police officers pushed past me calling his name.'

It was a fittingly inglorious end to a career of violence, brutality and murder.

Levi Bellfield was born on 17 May 1968 in nearby Isleworth. He was to live, work and carry out his acts of crime within that west and south-west area of London and the surrounding home counties that he knew so well. His mother Jean was the dominant force in his life. Even when he was behind bars years later he'd phone her as often as four times a day and she'd always bring him his favourite pork scratchings on visiting days. His father, Joseph, a car mechanic, died when Bellfield was eight and the youngster became an adored 'mummy's boy'.

After his father's death, Levi became close to his uncle, Charlie Brazil, in Surrey's gypsy community. Bellfield was brought up with two sisters, a brother and a number of step-siblings on a west London council estate and the children were told they should be proud of being Romany. That led to Bellfield boasting in later years of his 'pure' gypsy blood. It meant, he maintained, that he was superior to other races. Scholastically he made little impression either at Crane Junior School or Feltham Community School, before leaving at 16 to do casual work for a house clearance and removal firm.

After Bellfield moved out of the family home aged 22, rarely a day passed without his visiting his mother. But he entered into other relationships and by the time he was arrested he had at least eight children by three women – estimates of the total number of offspring varied from 11 to 13. It proved impossible to say accurately how many boys and girls he had fathered. He had many of his lovers at the same time: sometimes two women would be pregnant at once by him and the women in his life often knew one another. They would help each other when he was violent to one of them.

Bellfield picked up girls in nightclubs and had girlfriends in addition to his 'wives.' As the years passed he seemed increasingly fascinated with ever-younger women and eventually with young girls. He would drive around at night looking for runaways or girls getting off buses and he would tempt them by chatting them up or offering them drinks. He used a succession of vehicles often with darkened windows and his vans had carpets or mattresses in the back as well as a baseball bat.

One of the women in his life found a magazine with the faces of the blonde women in it slashed out. She later told police, 'He hates women, hated blonde women.' On the one hand Bellfield had a series of blonde lovers, yet he believed women who dyed their hair blonde were 'sluts', 'impure' and 'deserved to be messed around with'. He boasted to friends that he had shaved his entire body to avoid leaving any DNA evidence and was 'untouchable'. He also, according to one newspaper report later, acted as a police informant, passing on what was described as 'tittle-tattle'.

Women were simply objects to be propositioned. He also liked to carry cash and tried to impress his targets by getting lots of it out and showing it to them. Behind bars he told a cellmate what he really thought of women: 'You feed them and keep them – you can do what you want to them.'

It was a sentiment one of his ex-girlfriends recognised: 'He would start off extremely nicely, playing the fool and trying to convince them that he wasn't a threat. But once they trusted them, he turned into a controlling monster.'

Levi Bellfield – also known as Lee – had a criminal career which started at 13 with motoring offences, possession of an offensive weapon and assault. By 23, he had already served a prison sentence for hitting a police officer in the face when asked to turn down the music at a house party. He had grown up to be six feet tall and he weighed 16 stone even when he was young. On one shoulder he had a devil tattoo. Much of his bulk came from the steroids he used in bodybuilding. Despite his size, he had a rather high-pitched, almost effeminate voice, but he was proud of how he'd turned out. On the Friends Reunited website his entry read: '*Was short at school now over six feet ha ha… i havnt grown up still think im 18 out clubing, ibiza, tenereif. A bit flash like the labels am i sounding a prat???? dont look my age... any single girls out there e mail me.'*

Often when talking to girls he would use an alias – one estimate suggested that he had over 40 false names. He was later to claim that any false names were used purely 'for tax reasons' or to avoid people angry at his wheel clamping activities. Among the other identities were Levi Rabbets (a family name), Lee Johnson and David Bennett. His friends ironically called him 'Mr Truthful' – because he was a compulsive liar.

It was in 2000 that Bellfield decided to branch out from bouncer to the more lucrative world of clamping. Ricky Brouillard worked as a clamper with Bellfield and knew him when he was dating one teenage girl. Brouillard described him as an 'animal'. In a character statement given to police but never heard in court, he claimed the girl was 'naive' and Bellfield 'didn't treat her very well. Her sister was a tiny girl, 14 years old. He told me he had sex with her. She had long, blonde hair. I remember being disgusted. I met her on one occasion and he asked me, "Do you want to buy her off me?"' On one occasion Bellfield had sex with another teenager in front of Brouillard.

Bellfield suffered wild mood swings, worse, took anti-depressants and was to later claim that he had twice tried to kill himself.

Some victims of Bellfield's brutality had never met him before or knew him only in passing. Other women, however, lived with him and had his children. They were eventually to describe the horror of being part of his life. Emma Mills, whose home was raided that November morning when he was arrested, gave one of the most intimate glimpses into the psyche of the fiend. For years she had suffered both mentally and physically at his hands and she eventually talked in press interviews of his random brutality and violence. 'I always thought Levi was a player. He's a cheat, he's a bully, he's a liar but I never thought he'd killed anyone. Now, though, looking back, when the police told me [what he had done] I didn't instinctively say he hadn't. I don't think he'll admit to killing anyone. He's not the type to own up to anything. He's a control freak. Levi likes to have the power and control over everything and that includes women. Now, I feel such guilt for my children for giving them a father like that. They adore him and they've got to grow up with the knowledge and the stigma of what he's done. And I feel guilt for those girls. Every day I think about them. If I'd only realised, they might be alive.'

Emma, whose father was an insurance broker from Surrey, met Bellfield at Rocky's in 1996 when she was recovering from a bout of glandular fever. 'Everybody knew Levi. He was a bit of a cheeky chappy and always friendly and kind. I was quite impressed by him. He was very charming. One night I'd had too much to drink and Levi said, "Come on, babe, I'll take you home." He drove me back and dropped me off at the door and was the perfect gentleman. A few weeks later, he took me home again and this time we kissed. I was completely obsessed by him. He would leave flowers and notes at my house and was always calling me. He was my first proper boyfriend and he made me feel very special. For my 19th birthday he bought me a huge bucket of roses. At karaoke nights, he would sing, "You to Me are Everything". Even now, every time I hear it, I think of the one time I was happy, when I believed everything he said.'

After six months, Emma left home and moved in with Levi in the council house in Walton that he shared with his uncle Charlie. It was different from the life she had led – everyone smoked and drank all hours of the day and slept in their clothes. 'When the reality of the place hit me it was quite scary,' said Emma, 'but I loved Levi and it was exciting to be independent.' It was only a matter of weeks before another side of Bellfield's personality emerged, she said in lengthy interviews in both *The Mail on Sunday* and the *News of the World*. 'He'd been drinking and we had an argument because I'd asked for Uncle Charlie's help about something without Levi's permission. I was driving him home from the pub and he started hitting me on the side of my face by my left eye. Then the car ran out of petrol and we walked the rest of the way home. It was about two miles with him punching and kicking me the whole way … Levi called his ex-girlfriend Jo and told her to take me to hospital. He told me not to give my real name and I told them I'd been beaten up by a gang of girls. Afterwards, he cried and said he loved me. He was so sorry that I forgave him.'

A month later, she told both newspapers, they had a violent argument. She said, 'We'd had a row. I'd been out with friends and he didn't like it. A couple of nights later, we'd been out for a drink. I was driving us home when he ordered me down all these little roads. We got to Walton bridge and then he got the back of my hair and said, "You think you're going to get away with the other night?" Then he undid the belt of my jeans and said, "Next time I tell you not to do something, don't do it." Bellfield attacked her. 'Afterwards, I was in shock. The next day I still wasn't speaking to him but then I thought, Don't be dramatic, Emma ... Then I started to blame myself for the argument.'

Yet in the middle of this mayhem, she said, they 'did have nice times'. For her 21st birthday, he hired a limo and they stayed at the Waldorf and he took her to see *Saturday Night Fever*. 'I knew the relationship wasn't right because he was so possessive. My mum hated him but I was too proud to admit she was right. Then I was too frightened to leave him because I was afraid of what he might do to her. By then I knew what he was capable of. I just started to live my life in a way that wouldn't bring that side out, in a way that was acceptable to him.'

A year after they met she became pregnant and she stayed. She had no one to talk to – she said she no longer spoke with her mother or any of her old friends. 'I couldn't leave. I had no money, no job and no one but Levi.' She wanted to work but knew that Bellfield would not allow it. 'He never hit me again after that first time but sometimes he would slap me. And he'd always pull my hair and call me a "slag" and a "bitch". She added: 'It was like I'd become a possession. I don't know how I coped.'

Their second child was a boy born in 1999 and in the autumn of 2001 – six months before Milly disappeared – he made her act out a fantasy. 'On one occasion,' he got a camera out and said, "I know, let's have more fun." He started videoing me and made me perform for the cameras. Then he strangled me with my cardigan. I was terrified. I thought he was going to kill me.' The next day he was completely normal. 'I came down and he said, "Morning, babe." He went out to work and I rang my mum and said, "I want to go today." I packed the children's clothes into two bin bags and Mum got me into a refuge.'

But the two got together again and lived at 24 Collingwood Place, Walton, just a few yards from the spot where Milly Dowler was last seen alive. 'I believed that he'd changed. And he was true to his word. He never touched me again.' Emma said. 'He took me on holidays. He was no Prince Charming but that was a happy time for me and him.' Her evidence about what happened at the flat and the events in the days leading up to and after the disappearance of Milly were to play a crucial part in Bellfield's eventual trial, as we will hear.

On 4 February 2003, Bellfield killed Marsha McDonnell. While not behaving strangely after that attack, he decided to go away on holiday at short notice, a pattern he was to repeat. 'He did suddenly announce that we were going to Tenerife. We went to Tenerife three times that year, all last-minute holidays, but that was the only odd thing,' Emma later said. Even when Bellfield's own mother talked about a suspect who had just been arrested –

later released – in connection with Marsha's murder, 'he didn't seem any different'. In other words, he showed no reaction to events he had secretly played a part in. 'And he loved watching *Crimewatch*. He'd always watch it if it was on. I once found a pair of plastic surgical gloves in his coat but when I asked what they were for, he said it was to do with his clamping. I believed him.

'In July, he went really peculiar. He'd rented a flat in Hanworth and would go off all the time. Then he rang me one night and said he was so sorry for what he'd done to me. I thought he meant going off with other women because by then I knew he'd been having an affair with a local girl, Terri Carroll. He was edgy. He'd always had panic attacks but they got much worse. He was clammy all the time and wouldn't come round if it was daylight. He'd ring and say, "I'm parking now at the end of the road so open the door for me. He'd run along the road with his hood up and if I hadn't opened the door in time he'd practically kick it down. Then he'd go straight upstairs to the bedroom. And he had to have all the curtains closed."

On 19 August of the following year, Bellfield killed Amelie Delagrange. 'It must have been a few days afterwards that we had a fight. He asked me to turn the radio down and I said, "No," because the children were dancing to it. He got the stereo and threw it over [their son] Andrew's head and out of the front door. Then he went into the kitchen, smashed it up and went outside. I still ignored him but then every now and then I'd hear a thud from the garden. I thought he must be kicking the wall in temper.

Eventually I opened the door and asked Levi what he was doing. He came out of the shadows like something out of a horror film. There was blood pouring out of the side of his head. That was what he'd been hitting against the wall.'

At the end of August, she found Bellfield sitting on the bed, rocking back and forth and sobbing. She got the doctor to speak to him on the phone. Bellfield said he'd taken an overdose some days earlier and, as she had also found piping he bought to use in the car, Emma arranged for him to be taken to a psychiatric ward. 'I called a friend who took him to Hillingdon A&E. Levi called me from the hospital car park. He was crying and said, "You'll be burying me in a month. If not, I'll be in prison."' When she asked him why, he said it was over a fraud. 'To be honest, I didn't really know much about all his different deals. I turned a blind eye. And anyway, you didn't ask Levi questions. Then he said, "Just do me one thing, Emma. Always look after my children and make sure they're all right." That he could say that angers me like you wouldn't believe. He always said he idolised his children. Then how could he do this to these other families? I'm not sure we'll ever be able to understand it. He was a control freak.'

Bellfield refused to stay in hospital and instead arranged for them to go away for a holiday in Kent. He became the 'old' Levi Bellfield again and when they saw a television appeal for information about the killing of Amelie he turned to Emma and said of the presenter, 'F★★★★★★ wanker, I'd like ten minutes with him.'

When Bellfield was eventually arrested, Emma was left with the dilemma of what to tell their children. They had left the house in their pyjamas on the morning of the arrest. 'We never went back. At first, I tried to hide it from them. You want to cosset them from everything but that only made it worse. They were very, very hurt at the beginning. The nights I've cuddled them and they've begged me to see their daddy. That was when they didn't know what had happened. In the end, I told them on the advice of psychiatrists. And after Levi was arrested I started a diary for them so that they know what happened in years to come. I never ever want my children to tell me that I lied to them.' For them the man who callously took the lives of other parents' children was 'a kind and loving father'.

'That's why I can't understand how he could do this to these families. It's as if there are two different Levis. As the oldest, I think Anna finds it very hard. She doesn't go to bed at night, she can't be on her own, can't eat properly. She doesn't mention him. She still loves her daddy but doesn't feel that's allowed. But she can tell me every minute of every day how much she loves him. To the children he is still their daddy and, if they want to see him when they're older, I'll stand by them a hundred per cent. I do worry for them. And if we were still there with him I'd worry but we're in a completely different environment now. I just hope I'm doing the best I can. They're going to have a different upbringing now. I'm not Levi's mum bringing up Levi. They are amazingly resilient … Andrew said to me, "Is Daddy ever coming out of prison?" I said, "No," and he said, "That's good. You can't kill people and come out of prison." I may be free of him but I'll always feel guilt for those girls and their families.'

Emma Mills was not the first woman who had a 'relationship' with Bellfield, bore his children and also played a key role in his trials. Johanna Collings was in her early twenties when she met Bellfield in the mid-1990s. She witnessed his perversion and had to listen to his warped stories of power and sex. 'He was six foot of pure evil,' said Johanna. 'When he came in late after working on a club door, he'd tell me how he had "another little slut". Levi took great pleasure in telling me how they fancied a kiss and a cuddle. When he finished with the girls, he just told them to, "F*** off back into the nightclub." It was what Levi did for a hobby. He's a sick, serial murderer.'

Johanna experienced his violent side not long after moving in with him. 'He beat me and forced my face over the pictures of blondes, shouting, "I f****** hate blondes, they should all f****** die." He'd wrap his belt round my throat ... He'd make me do whatever he wanted. I'd be told, "Be a good little slut." Levi burnt cigarettes on me, beat me with pool cues and ashtrays, threw me down the stairs and even once took a claw hammer to my body. Once I ironed his trousers wrong for work and he went absolutely off his head.'

Johanna split with Bellfield in 1997 after discovering he had also been seeing Emma at the same time. 'I finally found the strength to get rid of him after years of his abuse. I told him I never wanted to see him again and he was out of the door. After everything he had done to me, I felt I could finally move on with my life. Now I'm ashamed to call him my ex and the father of my children. I believe in the Bible – an eye for an eye, a life for a life. He should hang and I would stand there, pull the lever and smile as he danced on the rope.'

Another to survive a relationship with Levi – just – was Terri Carroll. She was in her mid-teens when she met him in December 2003 outside her school in Hayes, west London. She had spent some of her youth in care and was studying for her GCSEs. Terri was introduced by a mutual acquaintance who worked with Bellfield as a clamper. 'I was instantly attracted to him. He told me he was 28 [at the time he was 35]. I thought it was cool that an older guy paid me attention. He was funny, charming and kind in the beginning. He would take me out for dinner, pay for taxis home and he bought me a mobile phone and presents. My self-esteem was very low and I quickly became infatuated with him. I didn't tell friends or family I was seeing him. I wanted to but he told me to keep it a secret and I went along with that.'

One of their earliest evenings was spent at a nightclub in Kingston where he had worked as a bouncer. She was impressed that he was able to jump the queue and then take her into the VIP area. 'He told me that he was separated from his partner and had a couple of kids. He seemed tough, yet nice,' says Terri. He bought her alcopops that night and then drove her to his Hanworth flat, before leading her straight to his bedroom. 'I didn't want to sleep with him, but he didn't listen. It was all over in a few minutes and we didn't even undress. I felt sick and cheap. I had slept with one boy before Levi but I was very inexperienced.' Nevertheless, Terri agreed to see him again. 'I was a stupid little girl. After a few weeks, he took me to a hotel room where again he got me drunk before we had sex. He kept hitting me and slapping me on my face and body while we were on the bed ...When he had finished, he called a male friend and told him to come round and that I would have sex with him. When I refused, Levi got so angry he punched me in the face. He said if I didn't do what he said he would dump me and find another girl. Luckily, his mate didn't turn up.'

Although many young women would have left Bellfield there and then, she did not. 'He was my first real boyfriend and I didn't want to lose him. But the love soon turned to fear. He made it clear he would kill me or hurt my family if I ever left him.' Terri agreed to move into Bellfield's flat just three weeks after meeting him and he commanded her to stop going to school. Shut off from friends and family, she spent up to 12 hours a day alone in Bellfield's dirty one-bedroom flat. She could not leave without his permission. 'He didn't want boys coming near me. If he rang me from work and I didn't answer he would accuse me of having someone in the flat. Before we got a landline installed, he would call me on my mobile and make me flush the toilet to prove I was inside. He abused me physically and verbally nearly every day. He would tell me I was fat and spotty and that no other man would even look at me. When I cried at his insults, he laughed and told me I should be grateful to have him. I was constantly on edge, never sure what mood he would be in when he came home from work. One minute he would be cuddling me and telling me he loved me, the next he would throw me to the floor like a rag doll.'

It was while he was living with her that he tried to kill schoolgirl Kate Sheedy and murdered Amelie Delagrange. All the while he was also still living with Emma and their children. Terri saw a change in him after what would have been the second attack that August. 'He shaved his head and started drinking heavily in the mornings. He left me at my mum's house for three weeks, telling me he had to get away for a while because someone was after him. I knew not to ask questions but I felt devastated and rejected.' Bellfield eventually returned to the flat with Terri. Another three months of terror and fear followed.

On 22 November 2004, Terri was spending the night at her parents when she was woken up by the sounds of armed police hammering down the front door looking for Bellfield. That night, however, he was staying with Emma Mills. 'I told them where he was. A few hours later they returned to tell me he'd been arrested on suspicion of murder. I knew he was capable of doing bad things, but I was stunned. I still loved him. Even after what he put me through I wanted to be with him. He would call me from prison, telling me that the police had got the wrong person and laughing about the compensation he was going to get. I wanted to believe he was innocent, but I knew what he was capable of. But after a year, the reality of how evil he is sank in and I couldn't bear to speak to him again, so I changed my number. He was coming home and getting into bed with me with the blood of those girls on his hands, I'm plagued by flashbacks of the night he nearly added me to his list of victims. I will have to live with the memories of what he did to me but I am just grateful I managed to escape alive.'

Terri Carroll's time with Bellfield was fleeting. The same could not be said for Becky Wilkinson, who had four children by him during the course of their much earlier relationship. She was a 19-year-old, blonde barmaid with a child when she fell for the smooth-talking Bellfield back in 1989. 'He was a real charmer. I thought he was a nice bloke. But he ruined my life … Everything was fine at first. But it was after we had our first child Bobbie that things went bad. For five years I went through a traumatic, violent relationship with Levi that I couldn't escape.'

They were only a few months into their relationship when she first became pregnant. 'He was a control freak. He felt having all these children made him look a big man. The night I went into labour, it was snowing and we didn't have a phone but he would not take me to hospital. I had to walk to a phone box and call my mum to take me. Two days after I got home, he kicked me down the stairs. He began hitting me and bringing other women back to the house when I was out … I wasn't allowed to speak to my family or see them. He wouldn't let me do anything. When he was arrested and let out on bail [on charges unrelated to the later murders], I just felt I had to constantly look over my shoulder. I didn't sleep.'

At the time Bellfield was still living with his mother. 'He is a real mummy's boy,' Becky said 'He once joked that she wiped his bum until he was 12 … He could do no wrong in her eyes. I was young and naive and, when he hit me, he would say "Sorry" afterwards and I would forgive him.… I kept trying to leave and when I eventually did he would still stalk me … He has never left me alone. It has been a nightmare.'

Even after the arrest he continued to be an influence. 'Our eldest tried to take an overdose because she was being bullied at school over her dad. They are ashamed they are related to him.' Bellfield wrote from prison for pictures of their four daughters, Bobbie, Jess, Hannah and Jaynie. 'I felt quite sick when I saw it because I knew straight away who it was, from the writing.' Becky said that in the letter he said he was sorry for the 'grief' he had brought on them and that he had said, 'I know I am not an angel. But what's done is done. We can't turn the clock back. I am going to ask you a favour, if you could find it in you to send me some pictures of you and the kids. I'd love to say you and the girls are my family and I mean that but do I have the right? Don't write me a nasty letter, I beg you, I am at the lowest of low, please, please understand. Levi.' Bellfield added, 'Promise you'll never show anyone this letter.'

Yet Bellfield's own teenage daughter Bobbie too had been a

victim. She had seen him at Christmas in 2002, two months before he bludgeoned Marsha to death. 'Levi was never a proper dad. He didn't show any signs of care and affection. I never remember him working but he always had cash. He wouldn't give Mum any money at all. And he only ever gave me one present. It was a Barbie doll on my sixth birthday. He called me "Daddy's favourite girl". I don't think he bought my sisters anything at all. One time he put some powder on to a spoon and told me to eat it because it tasted nice. When I did my mouth felt like it was on fire. He'd given me mustard powder. He started laughing, saying, "That can't hurt you!" but I was in tears. I also remember him giving me vodka telling me it was water and he made me light cigarettes for him.'

Her father used to leer at girls she knew as he drove her to school. 'He would wind down the window and shout comments like, "Look at the arse on her" and "Hello sexy",' she said. 'Knowing what I know now he was probably thinking of all kinds of horrible things he'd like to do to them. It's hard to comprehend that a father would do that in front of a child. It shows what a twisted mind he has. Mum was always terrified of him. Mum must have said something to upset him. He picked up what was closest at hand – which was a bike wheel – and whacked her on the back with it. Then he grabbed a brick that had fallen off the wall and hit her with that too. She was shouting for him to stop and I started screaming.'

Bobbie also remembered her mother Becky started seeing

another man after the couple split. 'Mum got home and found all the windows downstairs smashed to pieces. A neighbour said he had seen a man breaking them all with a hammer but he couldn't identify him. Mum and I knew it was Levi though. He was just letting Mum know he wasn't happy about her new man.'

He was open about his own new relationship and Bobbie would sometimes be around Emma on nights he was supposed to look after his daughter. 'He drove me to Emma's flat one night. No one was in. He didn't have any keys so he tried to make me climb through a window to let him in. I refused because there was a dog in there so he broke in by opening the lock with a coat hanger. Once inside he went straight to the bedroom and stayed there for several minutes while I went to play with the dog. It was all very sinister and it chills me to the bone to think about what he might have been doing.

'He used to beat up Emma like he beat up my mum. I once heard her screaming in a next-door room, "No, Levi! No!" Afterwards, her face was red and swollen. But I knew he would never lay a finger on me. He was always trying to impress and intimidate me, not beat me up. While I was there he showed me a hammer, a knuckle duster and an air rifle – his "weapons". Mum eventually got a court order to get me out of there and came to pick me up. Levi applied to get access to see me one day in the week and on a Saturday but I refused to see him.'

The day after the arrest, police began to dig up the back yard at Little Benty using drills to smash through paving. Forensic teams then went in to analyse objects in the ground and took away two sofas. They were also granted an extra 36 hours to question Bellfield, who was charged with three rapes on 25 November and remanded in custody. It was more than a year later, on 2 March 2006, Bellfield was charged with the murder of Amelie and the attempted murder of two other women. He was due to appear in court the next day, a spokeswoman for the Crown Prosecution Service said. Bellfield was also charged with the attempted murder of Kate Sheedy.

There were two more cases to be taken into consideration. There was an accusation of attempted murder and of causing grievous bodily harm to a 33-year-old hairdresser, Irma Dragoshi. She had suffered serious injuries after being struck from behind with a blunt object. The attack was alleged to have taken place in the village of Longford near Heathrow on 16 December 2003. Irma was waiting for a bus at 7.45pm and there was one other woman waiting nearby. Mrs Dragoshi was attacked as she talked to her husband and woke up in hospital the next day with a huge lump and a wound to her head.

The other charge was that of attempted abduction and false imprisonment of a teenager, Anna-Maria Rennie, on 15 October 2001. The alleged victim, then 17, was at a bus stop in Hospital Bridge Road in Twickenham, west London, on her way home. She was approached at 11.30pm by two men in a dark-coloured Ford Mondeo who tried to bundle her into a car but she screamed and managed to escape.

Dominique and Jean-Francois Delagrange sat only a few feet from Bellfield as he was formally charged with their daughter's murder at Bow Street magistrates' court. Flanked by three security officers he spoke during the nine-minute session only to confirm his name and that his date of birth was 17 May 1968. He clapped as he was remanded in custody. That was the attitude he was to display whenever he appeared in a court, dismissive of its authority, contemptuous of any sense of justice

After the brief hearing, Mr Delagrange said, 'We have every faith in the British justice system. The British police have been excellent and kind. It has been difficult and emotional but it was important to be here in memory of our daughter.'

Dominique added, 'It's difficult to describe our feelings at the moment, we can't really say more at the moment. It is Amelie who gives us our courage to be here today.'

Bellfield, who did not apply for bail, was scheduled to appear at the Old Bailey on 31 March and on that date, when he appeared via a video link, he was further remanded until 9 June. In late May, it was announced he would be charged with the murder of Marsha McDonnell. So on 26 May he appeared at Bow Street magistrates' court and faced the additional charge. As he left the dock, a member of the public called out to him, 'You f★★★★★★ beast!' and he replied, 'Get the right person, mate!'

Bellfield appeared by video link from Woodhill Prison, Milton Keynes, on 9 June and his trial was fixed for April the next year. It was later put back until October 2007. DCI Colin Sutton said,

'The case has been adjourned at the defence's request to give them more time to gather evidence.'

The streets of west London had at last been saved from his evil presence. Police had had him under surveillance for some time before their dawn raid and, the very day before they burst into his house, horrified officers had seen him drive up to a bus stop in broad daylight and start talking to two young girls. They later told the police that he had offered them a lift and asked how old they were. When they said they were 14, he drove off after saying, 'You must be virgins. I bet you are nice and tight.'

CHAPTER 7

ellfield's trial began at the Old Bailey on 12 October 2007. It was to last five months, a lengthy period of time, even for a case of such seriousness. Bellfield pleaded not guilty to all the charges he faced: murdering Marsha McDonnell and Amelie Delagrange and the attempted murder of Kate Sheedy. There were also the more recent charges – the attempted murder of Irma Dragoshi, causing Mrs Dragoshi grievous bodily harm with intent and the attempted kidnap and false imprisonment of Anna-Maria Rennie.

It was the first time the world at large had heard of the exact nature of Bellfield's dark deeds. The opening speech from prosecutor Brian Altman merits repeating in part, even though we have already touched upon some of the events the hushed courtroom heard him describe. We can then look at what the witnesses and victims said during the case.

Mr Altman began by telling the court: 'Between October 2001 and August 2004, five women – four of them young women aged between 17 and 22 – were violently attacked. Two of these young women were brutally murdered by being battered about the head with a blunt instrument. One young woman survived a horrific attack on her when she was driven at and run over. Another woman suffered a nasty injury when she was struck on the head. Another woman survived attack without injury … The prosecution case is that Levi Bellfield was the attacker.'

Mr Altman said the attacks began in October 2001 when the defendant emerged from a car in which there was another man and approached Ms Rennie. She was walking in the street late at night after a row with her boyfriend, said Mr Altman. She was declining the defendant's invitation to go with him when he physically picked her up from the ground and sought to drag her to the car from which he had emerged. 'She was fortunate enough to escape injury.'

Marsha McDonnell was attacked in February 2003 when she left a bus near a stop close to her home in Hampton after an evening out with friends. 'She was struck on the back of the head with a blunt instrument as she approached the house. She died later in hospital,' said Mr Altman.

In December 2003, Irma Dragoshi was attacked at a bus stop in the village of Longford, near Heathrow airport. Mr Altman said, 'The defendant got out of a vehicle and ran over. He attacked her by hitting her with a blunt instrument.' Mrs Dragoshi had recovered but the injury left her with amnesia.

Kate Sheedy was attacked in May 2004 as she was making her way home after an evening out with friends. 'She got off a bus in Isleworth. She became suspicious of a people carrier vehicle which was stationary in front of her. In order to avoid that car from which she felt threatened she crossed over the road. Suddenly but very deliberately, the waiting people carrier moved, turned at speed and drove towards her. It ran her over in the mouth of the side turning, causing her massive injuries from which she survived, albeit with that she remains scarred mentally and physically.'

Amelie Delagrange, living in the UK to improve her English, was attacked in August 2004 in Twickenham. She too had spent the evening with friends. Mr Altman said, 'She took a bus home and missed her stop. She was walking up Hampton Road. As she was crossing Twickenham Green, she was attacked and hit over the head with a blunt instrument. She died from her injuries.'

Mr Altman told the jury, 'There are such similarities between the offences that the chances of them having been committed by two or more men working independently can safely and sensibly be excluded, such that all the offences were the work of one man and that man was Levi Bellfield.' He said there was direct evidence linking Bellfield to the attacks on Anna-Maria Rennie and Irma Dragoshi, and 'compelling' circumstantial evidence linking him to the other three crimes. Ms Rennie identified Bellfield as her attacker when police reinvestigated her case following his arrest in November 2004, Mr Altman said.

The attack on Mrs Dragoshi was witnessed by one of the other people in the car that Bellfield used. Sunil Gharu, a 'friend and associate' of Bellfield, said Altman. Mr Gharu had said he saw Bellfield run out of the car and attack a woman standing at a bus stop, the court was told, but did not see him hit her over the head. He said he thought Bellfield was going for the victim's handbag but nothing was stolen from her, Mr Altman said. Mr Gharu said it appeared Bellfield 'spun her round' and she fell to the ground, banging her head. But nearer the time of the incident, Mrs Dragoshi said she had been struck over the head by her attacker and the injury to her head was not caused by a fall to the ground.

After his arrest, Bellfield attempted to turn the tables, claiming Mr Gharu had carried out the attack, but Mr Altman said the accounts provided by Mr Gharu and the victim provided 'powerful direct evidence' that Bellfield was responsible. It was open to jurors to use any findings in relation to one allegation to inform their verdicts upon the others, he added. 'The prosecution say the chances that these offences were committed by anyone other than Bellfield are so fanciful that you may reject them,' said Mr Altman.

He said the cases of Ms McDonnell, Ms Delagrange and Ms Sheedy were linked by the 'non-coincidental presence' at each of a vehicle associated with Bellfield: a silver Vauxhall Corsa, a white Toyota Previa and a white Ford Courier van. One of Bellfield's former landlords, Jason Woods, also ran a car finance company, and in November 2002 arranged the funds for Bellfield to get the silver Vauxhall Corsa. Mr Altman noted that the office of the car finance company was in 'the very same road in which Kate Sheedy was to be run over' and injured in 2004. The Corsa provided another significant link, the jury was told. 'It is of critical importance to the Marsha McDonnell murder in 2003. There is evidence that could conclude that it was the car that was driving down the road when Marsha McDonnell alone alighted from a bus after midnight.' CCTV footage showed a car of this description behaving in a 'curious manner'. Mr Altman said, 'It slows down as it approaches the bus from which Marsha is alighting,' and 'the behaviour of that car is identical to the behaviour of the people mover' which mowed down Kate Sheedy as she got off the bus.

Referring to the charges in total, Mr Altman said, 'He denies that he is responsible for any or all of these offences. It is his case that, if they were committed by the same man, it is not him or, if they were committed by different men, he was not one of them.' The jury were to visit the west London areas where the attacks took place. Bellfield 'lived and worked in south-west London most of his life and knew the area extremely well', Mr Altman said.

Anna-Maria Rennie, who was 23, had lived in Spain since July 2004 but came back to Britain in the year of the trial, said Mr Altman. She revisited the scene of her October 2001 attack, when she had gone for a walk at about 11.30pm to calm down after a row with her boyfriend. Mr Altman said she told police she remembered a car pulling up a few metres behind her. Looking back, she saw two men in a dark-blue Ford Mondeo. The one in the passenger seat got out and approached her.

She was visibly upset and crying and she believed she had told him about what happened with her boyfriend. Mr Altman said, 'She told police three days later that the man offered her a lift in the car, which she declined. She said a man of his age should not be offering young girls lifts … She began to walk away. She had only gone a few metres when the man grabbed her. He placed her in a bear hug which pinned her arms to the side. With his strength, he lifted her off the ground and tried to get her to the car. At the time, Anna-Maria weighed about seven-and-a-half stone. The man took her to the car in a very tight hold. Naturally, she was extremely scared. As he tried to get her to the car, despite being absolutely petrified, she kicked and struggled violently. It paid off because she managed to break away about one and a half metres from the car.' Then she ran home through a park and heard the man shouting after her something like 'whore', said Mr Altman. She told her boyfriend but did not report it to the police until later. She described the man as being about six foot and fat with tattoos on his arm. Jurors were shown pictures of Bellfield's tattoos – a boxing devil with the word 'Levi' on his right shoulder and a bulldog with a 'Tottenham FC' banner on his right leg.

Mr Altman said that, although Ms Rennie's recollection of

events had 'faded', one of the things she could recall was that she had been sitting at a bus stop at the time. 'In the context of buses and bus stops, this is an important feature when assessing the question whether these offences are all the work of one man.' After the arrest, Ms Rennie positively identified Bellfield in a video identity parade as the man who attacked her, he added. Bellfield remained silent when interviewed about the incident in September. Mr Altman said that, if Ms Rennie's identification was right, and there was 'no reason to believe that it is anything other than accurate', it proved that in October 2001 he was 'prepared to attempt to abduct a lone young female at night'.

Jurors were entitled to rely upon the evidence in the other cases to support the allegation and also upon the evidence in her case to support the others. Incidents had 'similar features' and there was a 'pattern emerging', Mr Altman said. The attacks involved 'the assailant using his vehicle in the hours of darkness to locate and target lone females who he then attacked'. Mr Altman said Bellfield prowled the streets in his car, peering into buses and checking out bus stops for lone women going home. 'The illuminations allowed the attacker of these women to see into the bus from the outside. These were not the chance victims of a street attack. They were the targets of a predatory man who had stalked buses and bus routes, looking for young women.'

Mr Altman also told the jury, 'Four of the victims were young women aged between 17 and 22 who were violently attacked. Two of these young women were brutally murdered by being battered about the head with a blunt instrument. One young woman survived a horrific attack on her when she was driven at and run over. One other woman suffered a nasty injury after being hit over the head. And another young woman escaped any harm by running off. The prosecution say that this defendant Levi Bellfield was the attacker in all these cases.'

When the trial resumed after a weekend break, Mr Altman said a pathologist thought 'a lump hammer was the possible weapon' in the attack on Marsha McDonnell. 'The evidence suggests a rapid attack with Marsha unable to use her hands for defence.' Mr Altman had told the jury that a silver Vauxhall Corsa car, which Bellfield owned at the time, was caught on CCTV footage from her number 111 bus. 'At the time of Marsha's killing, not only did the defendant own the Corsa but he was still driving it – not only up to and in the week before the murder, but shortly afterwards, when he sold it on,' said Mr Altman.

Six days before the murder, police spoke to a man of Bellfield's description in the car outside his sister's home. The man had a tattoo of a boxing devil similar to the one Bellfield had, he added. Mr Altman said Bellfield had sold the car in exchange for a van a week after Ms McDonnell's death. The prosecutor said the sale of the car was an 'act of desperation', as was Bellfield's decision to take his family on holiday to Tenerife shortly after the attack. He had told his partner at the time that the reason he wanted to take their daughter out of school to go away was because he was doing well in his clamping business and wanted some 'winter sun'.

Bellfield made no comment when asked under arrest about Ms McDonnell's murder in May 2005.

Mr Altman added that the attack on hairdresser Irma Dragoshi in December 2003 'proves the defendant's capacity for violent behaviour towards women'. Mrs Dragoshi, of Albanian origin, was 33, worked at a salon in Slough and lived in Hounslow. She was dropped off by her boss at a bus stop near Heathrow after finishing work at around 7.20pm on 16 December. At that time in winter, it was dark and quiet with no one around.

Mrs Dragoshi remembered taking a telephone call from her husband and telling him that her bus was late. She had her hood up and was facing the direction of the nearby White Horse pub, the court heard. 'This is the last memory she now has of the evening,' said Mr Altman. Her next clear recollection was waking up the next day in hospital suffering from terrible dizziness. There was a lump on the back of her head and her face was 'black and blue and swollen'.

Her husband Astrid Dragoshi recalled that he had been speaking to his wife on the phone when the call was interrupted. 'Quite suddenly, during the course of their conversation, Mr Dragoshi heard his wife scream and the telephone went dead,' said Mr Altman. Astrid called his wife back and the phone was answered by an English woman who passed it back to Mrs Dragoshi. She told him that she was in a great deal of pain and had been hit behind the head, the jury was told. Mr Dragoshi called the emergency services and headed to the scene in a taxi, where he found his wife sitting in an ambulance with her head in her hands.

Mr Altman said that since that night she had no recollection of what happened or conversations she had and she had been diagnosed with temporary amnesia. The landlord of the White Horse found her lying on the ground crying, speaking a foreign language. A police officer who arrived at the scene said Mrs Dragoshi had described waiting at the bus stop when a man approached her from behind and tried to take her mobile phone. When she struggled, he hit her on the back of the head.

Sunil Gharu, an associate of Bellfield who worked part-time for his clamping business, was in a car with him that night, the court heard. He recalled Bellfield parking the black VW Golf at the side of the road and turning off the engine and the lights. 'Suddenly Bellfield said, "Watch this." He got out of the car and, as he did so, told Gharu to jump in the driver's seat and Gharu did so. He saw Bellfield jog over to a woman standing at the bus stop. As he did so, Bellfield pulled up his hood,' said Mr Altman. Mr Gharu said Bellfield grabbed the woman's shoulder bag, spinning her around and smashing her to the floor. Mr Gharu said Bellfield then returned to the car and took over in the driver's seat. 'Bellfield got back in the car, turned on the engine but not the lights and drove off laughing,' Mr Altman said. 'During the journey they didn't speak about what Bellfield had done.'

Mr Altman added, 'You may think that, when he left the car boasting, "Watch this", there was an element of bravado, showing off to Gharu, demonstrating his capacity for unprovoked, wanton violence towards a woman.' When police questioned Bellfield about the attack in April 2005, he issued a prepared statement denying any involvement, but then issued a new statement when confronted with the evidence of Mr Gharu. This was a mirror image of what Mr Gharu had said, with Sunil as the attacker rather than Levi. Bellfield said he saw the other man get out of the car and pull at the woman's handbag. He noticed the woman falling to the ground and was 'shocked', did not want to be involved and drove off, he claimed.

Mr Altman told the jury of the attempted murder of Kate Sheedy after she left a bus near her home in Isleworth in May 2004. Mr Altman said she was not blonde like the first two victims but did have light-coloured hair. She had taken a short journey on the bus and was the only one to get off at her stop. 'There was no one else around, although she saw a car driving past. She got her keys out ready to let herself in to her home and then she heard an engine.' She looked up and saw a Toyota Previa people carrier parked in a side road. 'The engine was running but there were no lights on. It was a white people carrier with blacked-out windows. Kate sensed that something was not right about this vehicle and, sensing that, she crossed over the road to the other side. She did not like it. Something told her something was not right. What Kate was not to then know was that the people carrier had been stalking her before she even got off the bus. What the occupant of the vehicle was now doing was that, having noticed her on the bus and stopped with the engine running and no lights on, was to engage her.

'As it tragically turned out, Kate's instincts about the vehicle were right. As she reached a traffic island in the middle of the road, the car switched its lights on, revved up its engine and drove off. But it came back without warning. It did a U-turn and drove directly at Kate. She attempted to make a dash to the pavement but the car got to her before she could avoid it. It struck her and drove over her but that did not suffice. It reversed back over her before making off in the direction in which it came. Local residents heard a bang followed by a scream but thought little of it, living as they did near a pub. Gravely injured and in pain, she tried to crawl home. When she could go no further, she managed to phone her mother from her mobile phone, which she recovered from the road surface, and she had the presence of mind to call an ambulance.' After her life-saving operations, she had follow-up surgery and physiotherapy to help her walk again. She still suffered from lower back pain and spasms and had an uneven collarbone. Physical and psychological injuries remained. She had missed her A-levels because of what had happened to her but was granted her predicted results by the exams board. When she started university in October 2005, it was a year later than her friends, the court heard.

The jurors were shown Ms Sheedy taking part in a police reconstruction of the attack, filmed in snow in February 2005. She was seen to walk from the bus stop to the spot where she was run over. The young woman remembered the car that attacked her being white with blacked-out windows and that the driver's mirror was 'defective in some way', Mr Altman added. She recalled 'two shapes' being in the vehicle, one with short hair and broad shoulders and the driver having his arms forward across the wheel.

Jurors were shown a CCTV picture of a driver identified as Bellfield driving another vehicle with his arms over the steering wheel. And Mr Altman said Bellfield's former partner remembered that he would 'hold on to the steering wheel and he would rock'. The jury was shown CCTV footage of a Toyota Previa driving towards and then away from the scene of the attack. An expert said the vehicle that Bellfield was driving at the time was the same make and model as the one in the CCTV footage and there were 'no significant differences' between the two. They both had blacked-out windows, which were not a standard feature on a Previa, the jury was told. There was also evidence that Bellfield had the car that was associated with him valeted in June 2004.

The jury was shown images, believed to be filmed by Bellfield's then girlfriend, showing him saying 'f★★★ off' to the person recording and carrying a torch in his hand, just one-and-three-quarter hours after the attack. When shown the video by police, he said, 'Oh please.' Mr Altman said, 'He said that what had happened to Kate Sheedy had been despicable and he added, somewhat curiously, "I am showing remorse." He explained that by saying [it] he found it a sad thing to have happened. He said he wasn't too bright with English vocabulary and what he meant was he was disgusted that he was being accused of this crime.'

Mr Altman said the driver of the Previa had adopted the same system of stalking a bus as the driver of the Corsa who allegedly attacked Marsha McDonnell. 'It is the commonality of system that shows that this must have been the work of one man,' Mr Altman said. 'It is true that no blunt instrument was used to strike Kate over the head but, if the prosecution is right, he used a different blunt instrument to attack her – that was the blunt instrument of the car. This terrible crime was the work of none other than Levi Bellfield.'

Amelie's parents Jean-Francois and Dominique sat in court as details were given of their daughter's murder. Mr Altman said Amelie, blonde and 5ft 4in tall, was passionate about English and had arrived in Britain in April 2004 to further her studies. After drinking with friends in Twickenham on 19 August 2004, Amelie missed her bus stop and was killed as she walked home along Twickenham Green: 'She had been battered about the head with such severity that it caused her a massive head injury and she died from it. She had been struck on the back of the head with a blunt instrument and, like others before her, had been left for dead. Like the others, the attack was motiveless.'

Mr Altman said she had drunk three or four glasses of white wine and told a friend she felt a little bit drunk because she was not used to drinking. He added, 'It is not clear why Amelie missed her stop. It may be she was somewhat tipsy or it may be that the bus was travelling too quickly. She unexpectedly found herself getting off at the alighting stop.' She was battered to death during the eight minutes when Levi Bellfield's white van was parked by Twickenham Green. Bellfield had spotted her walking along and looking lost after getting off at the wrong bus stop. He followed her as she took a shortcut to her home along the Green and battered her over the head with a heavy object. He drove to Walton bridge and threw some of her possessions in the river. They were later recovered by police divers, said Mr Altman. Her bag contained a sim card, her purse, a CD player and two mobiles – one of which had registered with its network in the Walton area 22 minutes after she had last been seen. A CCTV camera spotted the van driving in nearby Sunbury in the direction of West Drayton where Bellfield was living at the time. The court was shown the images of Amelie walking to the Green in Hampton Road – and of the van said to be following her. At one point near a zebra crossing, the van was 42 seconds behind her and was later parked at the Green when she was last spotted just after 10.00pm.

A local resident told police he heard a female voice coming from the Green. 'It was a ten-second shout which included a scream,' said Mr Altman. The van moved off at 10.08pm and was seen in Sunbury 26 minutes later. 'In the intervening minutes, the van with Bellfield at the wheel had taken a necessary detour. He stopped in Walton bridge where he disposed of some of the items he had stolen from Amelie before or after the attack. They were items which were fished out of the Thames under Walton bridge. Only Amelie's killer could be responsible for disposing of the items in the river.'

Mr Altman said the van had been seen 'cruising' the area before the attack. It stopped suddenly at the Green. 'He had spotted Amelie sometime along her route and had become determined to engage her. He stopped with time to wait for her to catch up. He followed her across the Green, attacked her and stole her possessions and drove off. Amelie was a young female having just got off a bus having missed her bus stop. She was looking lost and was a bit tipsy. She was walking along alone and she had made herself a vulnerable target to a predatory male looking for someone just like her.'

The court heard that, in the weeks following the murder, Bellfield suffered from panic attacks and said to a friend, 'You don't know what I've done.' Bellfield also got rid of the van which has never been found. When police arrested him at his home in November 2004, they found a newspaper cutting about Amelie's death in a drawer.

On 19 October, the first woman to have been attacked by the bus-stop stalker and who survived to tell the story, Anna-Maria Rennie, gave evidence.

She told how she had been living with her then boyfriend Richard Lewison when, probably crying, she left after a row. After a while, she paused by a bus stop for about five minutes then continued walking along before turning around to come back. She spotted a man coming towards her and, feeling uneasy about him, she crossed the road. Her attention was attracted by the driver of a passing car: 'Somehow, I can't remember why but we had a conversation for about ten minutes.' She remembered him asking her if she wanted a lift home which she declined. 'After the conversation I started to go off and while he was still walking with me I must have turned around. He put his arm around me. I screamed, he had his hand over my mouth and picked me up off the floor. He had his left arm around me and his right hand across my mouth. He was very strong. He was walking me towards the car which was parked in a layby with the back passenger door open. I put up a big struggle. I was using everything trying to get my arms free, kicking, anything I could to get away. It was hard. I was being held very strongly towards him and the more force I was using to get away, the more pressure there was being put on me to keep there.

'He shouted, "You're a whore! You're a slut!"' Her attacker lifted her up and walked to the car. Anna-Maria said, 'I'm kicking, moving, screaming as much as I can to get away. Just before he gets to the car he lets go.' She said she had been shown various men on a video line-up, and that she had asked to see two of them again. She then chose Bellfield and said, 'He was the man.' She said the attack had 'changed who I am. I have always been a very open, confident person and for a long time afterwards it destroyed that. I was very withdrawn and quiet, I'm not so confident, I'm a lot warier.

The jury also heard of the night that Marsha McDonnell was found dying in the street near her home. Father-of-two David Fuller was woken late at night in February 2003 by a 'loud thud' which sounded like a car door slamming in front of his house but saw nothing unusual as he looked out of his bedroom window in Priory Road, Hampton. He began drifting back to sleep about 15 to 20 minutes later but heard moaning and spotted a pool of blood by a pillar near his front garden. He woke his wife, Bernadette. She told the jury, 'I could see a pool of liquid running down the pavement. When I looked again there was a hand stretched out from the pool so we knew there was somebody there, not just blood from the pillar.'

Mr Fuller called for an ambulance and kept the line open to hear advice from the operator as the couple rushed outside to help. Mrs Fuller told the court: 'She was face down with her arm underneath her. Her arm was stretched out in front of her and she clawed her arm backwards. It was quite difficult to see. She was obviously bleeding quite a lot. It was quite matted through her hair.' Towels were fetched on the advice of the ambulance operator and the couple tried to see where the blood was coming from. Mr Fuller recalled seeing the long-haired teenager lying face down 'on the floor obviously bleeding' when he first went outside. He told the court, 'She was still moaning at that point and my wife was still trying to talk to her. Her hand was on the ground and I think there was some movement in her fingers, in her right hand.' Mrs Fuller said, 'Initially she made a low moaning sound but that stopped quite soon when I was first out there.'

Irma Dragoshi too had to relive her ordeal in front of the jury and she struggled to cope with her emotions as she told of the moment she was struck on the back of the head at a bus stop. She had come to Britain with her husband Astrid in 1999 but had now returned to Kosovo. On the night she was attacked, Mrs Dragoshi was given a lift to a bus stop on her way home from work in Slough. Giving evidence from behind a screen at the Old Bailey in order to avoid eye contact with Bellfield, she described how her husband had called her on her mobile phone while she waited. 'He used to ring me every night asking me where I was and did I finish work. The next thing, I was in hospital.' She said she came round between 11.30am and midday. 'I had a very big lump in the back of my head. It didn't fit in my hand. I was trying to touch it but it was really very, very painful. It was so big. It is still there, you can feel it,' she said. The next day in hospital she was in 'strong pain' and could not open her eyes. Pain was coming 'from the back of my head and forwards from inside' and she later suffered headaches.

'How long did those headaches go on for?' asked Mr Altman.

'I still have it even now, a long time,' she replied.

Clifford Hare, landlord of the White Horse pub, near where the attack took place, told the jury how he discovered Mrs Dragoshi lying on the floor with a bump 'as big as an egg' on the back of her head. He described how he was walking home when he saw what 'looked like a roll of carpet lying in the bus stop. It moved. That's when I realised it was somebody lying there,' he said. 'She was in distress and was hurt. She was crying and confused. I helped her to her feet.' He said she was talking in 'broken English' and he did not understand her. The court was played a recording of his 999 call, in which her wailing and crying could be heard in the background. Mr Hare was telling the operator she had been mugged and when a bus arrived at the stop she wanted to go and sit on it, where she could feel safe.

Detective Constable Nick Deakin, who was the first officer on the scene, said Mrs Dragoshi was sitting next to the driver when they arrived. 'There was a lady who was complaining she had been struck on the head. She was in quite a hysterical state and was crying. It was difficult to establish what had happened. She pointed to an incredibly large bump on the back of her head. I had never seen anything like it.' He told the court how Mrs Dragoshi passed out several times on the way to the ambulance and became progressively less coherent.

Astrid Dragoshi, speaking through an Albanian interpreter, told the court how he called his wife as he waited for her to return home. They were having a 'normal conversation' as he asked her how her day had been and whether she felt tired after work. Then, he said, 'My wife started screaming. The phone was immediately off. There was no connection ... Of course, I was very worried, because if you hear your wife scream somewhere far away and you have not been able to help her, of course, how will you feel?'

Asked by William Boyce QC, defending, if he felt scared when he heard the screams, he said, 'My hair went up.' He said he tried ringing back several times until eventually he got through and an English woman passed the phone over to Mrs Dragoshi. 'She was screaming and she was also saying, "Someone has hit me on the back of my head,"' Mr Dragoshi said. 'She said, "I am in a lot of pain" and these were the words she was using: "I am in pain! I am in pain! I am in pain!"' Mr Dragoshi phoned for the police and an ambulance and took a taxi to go and see his wife.

'I told the driver to rush a bit because of what has happened,' he said. When he arrived at the scene emergency services were already there and he went to speak to her. 'She was repeating the words, "Someone has hit me at the back of the head and I am in pain." It seems that she was shocked and lost,' Mr Dragoshi said. 'I saw a big bump at the back of her head.' He accompanied his wife in an ambulance to hospital where a doctor spoke to her about what had happened.

Mr Altman asked Mr Dragoshi if his wife's memory had suffered later. The husband replied, 'The next night it was midnight and she asked me, "What are we doing here? Why are we here?"'

Sunil Gharu said Bellfield had told him, 'Watch this,' before throwing Mrs Dragoshi to the floor during the attack. 'He pulled up out of the blue. He switched off the headlights but the engine was still running. He made a comment like, "Look at this" or "Watch this" or something and said to me to get into the driver's seat. Then he got out of the car. He jogged up to where the bus stop is. I think he put his hood on, he had a hooded top on.' Bellfield then approached a woman wearing a long jacket and a scarf who was on her mobile phone, he added. 'It looked like he grabbed her. There was a bit of a struggle and he threw her to the ground then jogged off.' He said that Bellfield had grabbed the woman by the upper body and 'just sort of swung her' and had also been pulling on her handbag. Mr Gharu said that as she lay on the ground he jogged back to the car, took his place in the driver's seat and drove off. Mr Altman asked what Bellfield was doing as he drove away. 'Just laughing about what he'd done.' Afterwards the two men never spoke to each other about what had happened, he added.

More trauma awaited yet another of Bellfield's victims, Kate Sheedy, who relived the moment she was run over by the bus-stop stalker. Ms Sheedy, wearing a purple T-shirt and black cardigan, broke down in tears as she was cross-examined by Mr Boyce.

She told the court how she had been making her way home after celebrating her leavers' day at Gumley House Convent School. She organised a party for fellow sixth formers and had gone out later in Twickenham with friends, wearing a pink V-neck jumper, black knee-length skirt and pink shoes with a pink handbag. After taking the 22 bus home shortly after midnight and rummaging for her keys ahead of the two-minute walk home, she noticed the people carrier parked over the road. 'What drew my attention to it was the noise initially. Its engine was running and its lights were off. I knew it wasn't a vehicle that was normally there. It just made me feel nervous. I assumed it was a taxi dropping someone off or picking someone up, but there were no houses with lights on and I couldn't see or hear anyone. I felt very, very uneasy. I don't know what it was – a sixth sense, I don't know.

'I decided to cross the road so I wouldn't be walking directly past the vehicle. I was walking quite quickly. I had been made anxious and still didn't feel completely safe despite having crossed the road.' She was about to cross a small junction with an industrial estate service road as she made her way along the pavement when the car lights flashed and engine revved. The car drove past but then did a U-turn back towards her, she said. 'I thought the car was continuing, but instead of doing that it carried on into the entrance of the industrial estate. I was halfway between the little traffic island and the pavement and it drove straight towards me. It sounded and looked like it was trying to go as fast as it possibly could. I tried to run to the pavement. The car hit me. I was thrown to the ground lying on my front, so I was face down lying on the road. The car continued to move. It all happened very quickly. It drove straight over me. My head was under the car, but my legs were protruding out of the driver's side. Once the whole front wheel had driven over me it continued and then braked suddenly and then reversed so the wheel went back over me again.'

The vehicle carried on over her and then drove off. 'It was

going incredibly quickly,' she said. She gathered her phone, keys and handbag, which were scattered over the road. 'I phoned my mother to tell her I had been run over and I was around the corner and could she come and help me.' Ms Sheedy said she then called for an ambulance, which turned up 'after what seemed like an eternity … I tried to stand up. I stood up and fell straight back down to the ground again. I did try and shout for help but it was barely a whisper. Very little noise actually came out. I was determined I was going to get home. I didn't really realise I'd just been driven over twice. I continued to crawl a distance and then collapsed, at which point I realised I had very serious injuries.'

She told the court she suffered a collapsed lung, broken ribs and a broken collarbone in the attack. 'My liver was the most life-threatening injury. It was both crushed and fractured so couldn't actually function at that stage. I also had a very large laceration to my back. The whole lower bottom of my back had been ripped open.' She was unfit 'both mentally and physically' to start university that year and went instead the following October. She described how she was in 'an immense amount of pain' and found what happened to her 'hard to put into words'. 'For the first week I was kept unconscious, the pain would be too much for my body to cope with. There was a police officer constantly by my bed for the first week in case I died.'

The jury was read a statement by Eileen Sheedy. She had been at home when she said she was woken by a 'panicky' phone call from her daughter. 'Mummy, I've been run over, I'm in our road,' she said. The anxious mother ran out into the street but could not find her. 'I went back into the house as I felt I was having a bad dream. I checked the bedroom but it was empty. I tried to phone Kate on her mobile but it went straight to her answer phone.'

She went out to look for her daughter again but still could not find her and tried calling Ms Sheedy's father, James, and the girl's friend, Helen, before hearing the house phone ringing and running straight back inside. It was her daughter, saying, 'Mummy, where are you? Why is it taking so long? Come out of the house, keep going left, and you'll find me.'

Mrs Sheedy put the phone down and ran out. 'I saw a little body lying on the pavement near a parked car. I went over. Kate said to me, "I am on the phone to the lady from the ambulance and she needs to speak to you." The lady from the ambulance was telling me to calm down. I asked Kate how she was feeling. She said, "I am in a lot of pain, someone ran me over on purpose, it was definitely on purpose, he's a bastard." She said she'll tell me about it later.' Mrs Sheedy took off her jacket and put it over her daughter as she was cold. Then James Sheedy, who was separated from Mrs Sheedy, arrived.

Mrs Sheedy's statement continued: 'Kate told me she loved me. I said that I loved her and gave her a kiss. Kate was complaining of being in so much pain. Kate said, "If they don't get here soon I'm going to die." She was in so much pain. I was trying to comfort her.' Mr Sheedy flagged down the ambulance as it arrived, Mrs Sheedy said. 'Kate was asking for her dad and was extremely anxious and crying. She said, "I love you, Daddy, I love you, Mummy."' The parents got in the ambulance with her and went to hospital.

The court was also read part of the 999 call Kate made after being hit. She was asked 'Where does it hurt?' by the operator and replied, 'Everywhere. He ran over me twice ... The car stopped and checked me out ... I thought he was going to take me in his car but, when he saw that I knew he was dodgy, he just ran over me.'

Detective Constable Michael Jones told the jury how he spoke to Kate at West Middlesex hospital, just over an hour after she was run down. 'She was clearly in pain but surprisingly well enough to converse quite clearly,' Mr Jones said. She was wearing an oxygen mask and with her father by her side explained to the policeman in a 'clear voice' what had happened to her. He said she described her evening out and how she had been suspicious of the stationary vehicle.

Mr Altman asked the officer, 'What was her closing line to you?'

'Her closing line to me was, "Please get the bastard,"' Mr Jones replied.

The jury also heard of the initial error in the police hunt for Kate's attacker. Detectives investigating the near-fatal attack looked through security camera footage taken from a nearby pub, the County Arms. Initially, they only looked at three out of six tapes from the camera, missing the film that showed a white vehicle following the bus Ms Sheedy was on. It was not spotted until a complete review of the case was carried out some time later. Detective Sergeant Philip Royan said, 'The relevant part wasn't examined … The relevant part had a white vehicle following the bus and then driving off after Kate got off the bus. As I understand it, a number of tapes were seized – I think six in all. The officer who held responsibility took out some of the tapes and viewed them and said that they had been viewed and there wasn't anything of evidential value … I was none the wiser until a complete review of the case had taken place and it became apparent that the officer had only watched three of the tapes instead of the six.'

In relation to Kate Sheedy, the jury also heard from motorist Philip Lancaster, who saw a man he later identified as Bellfield in a white Toyota Previa with blacked-out windows the day before the attack. Mr Lancaster met him after having his own vehicle clamped in a pub car park in Bicester, Oxfordshire.

Then the full, heart-breaking details of Amelie Delagrange's young life and tragic death were told to the court. Her mother Dominique described her upbringing in France and her love for England. 'Amelie had a real passion for the English language which she would display from a very young age,' she said. 'She was a good student, sensible and never gave her parents any problems.' Ms Delagrange passed her baccalaureate exams 'with ease', then spent six weeks in Manchester as part of a language course. It was difficult for her mother. 'We were concerned at seeing her go abroad on her own. Parting was very difficult. But in due course Amelie returned, delighted with her training. 'After her happy experience in Manchester, she got it into her head to return to England.'

Mrs Delagrange said her daughter also spent six weeks in Alicante studying Spanish, 'but wasn't as happy as she had been in Manchester'. Then she took a job as a secretary before quitting in March 2004 to go to England and 'become truly bilingual'. She came to London and found a job as an assistant waitress at the Maison Blanc. 'She was happy and had a circle of French and English friends and she made good progress as time went on in England.'

Others spoke of Amelie's life in London. Boyfriend Olivier Lenfant said, 'She was a very sensible girl. She would never walk in places that would attract danger and she told me she would never walk down a subway on her own.' Her friend Lauren Pomares said, 'I would describe her as very friendly, quiet, very pretty, with a lovely smile.' Benjamin Batrix was one of the group who was with her on the night she died. He said, 'The conversation was that Twickenham was a safe area. We talked about other areas that weren't so safe.'

Gerald Renault was driving the 267 bus that Amelie took home. He described how she got off the bus at the end of the route at Fulwell bus garage. 'The French girl said to me, "Have I missed Twickenham Green?" I told her, "You have – it was three or four stops back."'

Mrs Delagrange wept in court and had to be comforted by her

husband as a pathologist described her daughter's fatal injuries. Dr Robert Chapman said, 'The death resulted from the effects of a severe head injury. There was a single, major, blunt impact injury to the back of the head that resulted in skull fracture, laceration and bruising.' The impact caused a 'crazy paving-style' fracture and he said there were 'similarities between the size and shape' of her wounds and those suffered by Marsha McDonnell. 'There is no evidence of any defensive injuries. The locations of the injuries would suggest a blow being struck from behind.' Dr Chapman said the three separate injuries to the front and back of the head and the number and severity of the wounds were inconsistent with a fall. He added, 'A blunt object such as a lump hammer or something of that sort could have been used to cause the injuries.'

Emma Mills, mother of three of Bellfield's children, was to play a great part in his trial four years later. But even in December 2007 her evidence, given from behind a curtain screen, was dramatic. She received a call in the middle of the night from Bellfield a few days after Amelie Delagrange was attacked in August 2004. 'He was really, really low – crying. He said he was going to kill himself,' she said. 'Around that time, he said he was in trouble with the police. He didn't pinpoint anything. He was quite vague, he was sobbing. He said he didn't have any money. He said, "I am in trouble with the police. I am going to go to prison." I was worried about him.' She wept as she said Bellfield told her to look after the children. 'He said to always tell the children that he loved them,' she said. The line went dead and she could not get back in touch with him. 'I think I spoke to him the next day but he brushed it under the carpet. He said, "Oh, it was the drink."'

Ms Mills talked of how their GP said Bellfield should go to hospital because he had told him he had taken an overdose. 'I phoned him. He was upset.' A friend took Bellfield to hospital and then she rang him again. She said, 'Levi said another couple of months and I would be arranging his funeral. Look after the children.' After only one night in hospital, he left and returned to Ms Mills' home in West Drayton. She said Bellfield then took her and the children, aged nine, five and six weeks, to visit a friend in Kent. Bellfield returned the white van he was driving to a pub car park and swapped it for another vehicle, she said.

Two friends of Bellfield told the Old Bailey how he broke down in front of them after one of the murders. Richard Hughes said the outburst occurred when he visited Bellfield and his partner Emma at their home. Bellfield was lying on the bed talking on his mobile and had obviously been crying. He said there were also beer bottles on the floor. Mr Hughes said, 'I knew he was pretty upset. He told me he needed some help. I said, "Do you want to go to the hospital?" He didn't want to go.' Mr Hughes left the house but returned a few hours later and drove Bellfield to Hillingdon hospital. During the drive, Bellfield rocked backwards and forwards. 'I said, "What's up, bruv?" He said, "You don't know what I've done." I left it at that. I think he did tell me that he had taken some pills.'

In January 2008, the trial entered its fourth month. Levi Bellfield was at last to give his version of events in a dramatic and lengthy appearance in the witness box.

CHAPTER 8

On Tuesday, 15 January 2008, Levi Bellfield took the stand in court five. He wore a dark-grey suit with a white shirt and a cream-and-pink tie. The answers to questions from his defending counsel William Boyce QC were delivered in that distinctive, high-pitched voice of his. The man known to friends as Mr Truthful because of his inveterate lying was about to try and talk his way out of his crimes.

He started by giving the jury some biographical details: that he grew up, worked and socialised in the Hounslow, Feltham and Hanworth areas and worked as a club doorman and then as a car clamper from 2002, running his own business. He employed around 50 men at various times and he had at least 20 vehicles a year. 'I don't know how many I owned and used,' he said. 'Everyone used them. Sometimes the key would be left on the wheel.'

Bellfield admitted he had made previous court appearances dating back to the age of 13. His offences had included taking a vehicle, having an offensive weapon and assaulting a police officer. He was jailed for a total of 13 months at Isleworth crown court in 1991 for hitting a constable in the face, common assault on a special constable and failing to surrender. Bellfield said, 'I was at a friend's house. The police came and told us to turn the music down. They turned it off. There was an argy-bargy and I was arrested.' In February 2005, he was jailed for eight months and banned from driving for seven years for dangerous driving after being stopped driving along a motorway hard shoulder at 70 mph. But Bellfield told the court it was the 'first time in my life' that he was giving evidence in court and he had never seen Anna-Maria Rennie before she appeared in court. 'No, never in my life,' he said in answer to the question.

He said he was angry and upset when he found out he was accused of the attacks. 'With all that's been going on with me regarding all these allegations, it knocked me sideways,' he said. 'I couldn't believe it.' He also had answers to his whereabouts on the nights of two attacks: Anna-Maria was assaulted on his son's birthday and he believed he was out having a Chinese meal. When Marsha McDonnell was brutally killed, he was 'pretty certain' he was at home watching Michael Jackson's interview with Martin Bashir on television. He answered, 'No, I was not' and 'Absolutely not' when asked if he was present at the scenes of the various crimes. But he did admit to being at Longford when Mrs Dragoshi was attacked.

'In relation to the incident involving Irma Dragoshi, were you in the vicinity at that time?' Mr Boyce asked.

Bellfield replied, 'Yes, I was.'

Mr Boyce asked, 'Did you yourself have anything to do with the assault on Mrs Dragoshi?'

Bellfield answered, 'No, I did not.'

It was, he said, one of his employees, Sunil Gharu, the man in the car with him, who carried out the attack. Bellfield did not know what was happening but was later sickened when he found out about her injuries, he told the Old Bailey. He had returned to his car to find Mr Gharu had got out. 'He was pulling at the lady. As he pulled a handbag or her arm, she fell back and that is when I drove off.' He demonstrated what happened in the witness box by using both his hands and pulling towards his chest. 'Part of me was in a bit of shock. I just did not want to get involved. I could not believe what happened.' He said Mr Gharu told him that he believed the woman had been involved in robbing his girlfriend of her mobile. 'I did not know Miss Draghosi's injuries. Looking at this lady's injuries now, I feel sick.'

Bellfield also said Mr Gharu and his brother were among about 20 men who had access to vehicles he had for his clamping business, and the brothers were using a Toyota Previa at the time schoolgirl Kate Sheedy was run over.

A few days after Amelie was murdered on Twickenham Green,

Bellfield said, he was feeling suicidal and depressed. He had taken 20 diazepam tablets the night before and he also told doctors he had bought a rope to hang himself. Mr Boyce asked Bellfield to confirm what he had told doctors at Hillingdon hospital on 25 August 2004. The clamper agreed he said he had been suffering from depression for two years and had become tearful and was experiencing panic attacks. After being admitted, Bellfield told doctors that he had tried to hang himself six months earlier but had taken the noose off. Three months later, he placed a tyre round his neck in another aborted suicide attempt. Bellfield said he had £20,000 in personal debts relating to cars he had bought and the home in West Drayton where Emma Mills lived with their children. She had given birth a month before to a baby which he did not want. Asked why he had discharged himself the next day, Bellfield said he had been affected by a teenage girl in the unit who was self-harming. 'I felt I was in a much better position than that girl,' he said.

Bellfield also touched on how he regretted living with Terri Carroll when his relationship with Emma Mills deteriorated. 'I dug myself a big hole getting involved with Terri,' he said. She had been texting him and threatened to knock his door down if he did not answer. Bellfield confirmed he had been arrested during the same year for benefit fraud.

After giving his evidence in chief, Bellfield was cross-examined by Mr Altman. One observer of that questioning said, 'It was fascinating to watch. Bellfield is the type of man who thinks he is smarter than everyone else. He met his match in Brian Altman.'

Asked by the barrister about the alias he said he used to avoid reprisals from people he clamped, Bellfield objected, 'I am here on trial for murder, not alias names.' He denied a claim by a couple in west London that he visited them in a white van hours before Ms Delagrange was attacked. His lengthy explanation was interrupted by Mr Altman asking him, 'Do you want to make a speech?' Bellfield later accused the couple of coming forward after seeing details of the vehicle in the *Sun* in order to get a 'day out at the Old Bailey', adding, 'I am sure they loved it. They are attention seekers,' he said as he apparently became more and more agitated. He also accused the police of trying to manipulate witnesses with their questioning. 'They are very clever,' he said.

Mr Altman suggested to him that he had 'massaged' his evidence and given fictitious accounts and Bellfield hit back by saying he had been asked a trick question and telling the prosecutor, 'I am not going to bite.'

The barrister asked him, 'You were cruising inside a van without any obvious destination, trying to pick up women who took your fancy – young, preferably blonde, attractive and alone. Preying on the bus routes?'

Bellfield answered, 'No, I was not' to each point.

He denied he had been 'on the prowl' or that it was him in a white Ford Courier van seen following Amelie Delagrange. Mr Altman, who at one point suggested Bellfield was a 'coward' for trying to shift some of the blame to his workers, said the attack on the French student took eight minutes. He asked, 'You had overtaken Amelie who you had spotted. You slowed down and you sought to engage her, lying in wait for her. Was the idea to get her into your van? As she crossed the Green, you got out to see, having tooled up with a hammer or some such. But she would not engage you and, in an outburst of sudden temper, you lashed out and hit her from behind. It was you and no one else but you who killed her. It was not enough to hit her once, you struck her again and possibly a third time.'

Bellfield denied the claims. 'The only thing I have done in these proceedings is to tell the truth.'

Mr Altman continued, 'Amelie rejected you and paid the price for that rejection.'

Bellfield replied, 'I have never met Miss Delagrange in my life.' He told the jury of seven women and five men, 'No airs and graces. This is me. I'm not trying to fool anyone. I'm not an angel, I'm not claiming to be an angel. But I'm not a killer. No way.'

He said he was 'outraged' by a suggestion during a police interview in May 2005 that he was 'out hunting' on the night Ms Delagrange was killed. That night, he claimed, he was looking at a second-hand car which was for sale and then went to a pub near his home.

Moving to the attack on Kate Sheedy, Mr Altman said Bellfield had been 'checking her out' and parked ahead of her so that he could see her in his wing mirrors. Then she crossed to the other side of the road. 'Did it anger you? It rather thwarted your plans, didn't it? What you did is you drove away, made a U-turn and drove back. You ran her over deliberately and reversed over her and sped away.'

'It wasn't me. I couldn't do that. It's senseless' he replied. And at one stage, accused of lying, he replied, 'I am fighting for my life here and I am doing my best.'

In his summing up, Mr Altman told the jury Bellfield displayed a pattern of behaviour before and after the attacks. 'It is the identical behaviour in each of these cases which says to you this is one man operating a system doing the same thing time and again.' He said in all the attacks the offender emerged from or returned to a type of vehicle which Bellfield was linked to at the time. 'Is that just plain bad luck, coincidence, chance or is it evidence that the same man is committing similar crimes?' asked Mr Altman. He also said all the offences took place at bus stops or after the victims had got off buses in an area Bellfield was familiar with. Similarities were drawn between the appearance and age of the women. 'The victims were young, alone, vulnerable, and extremely soft targets. They were all of a type.'

However, Mr Boyce accused the prosecution of 'cherry-picking' information to support the theory that all the attacks were carried out by one man. In his own summing up Mr Boyce said, 'A lot of this desperate squeeze is self-fulfilling. The police investigators have chosen the offences and chosen what to put in their theory.' He said there was no material to show how it was decided these five cases were linked to one man. 'It is cutting and pasting with no regard for consistency and no regard for accuracy – trying to fit the squeeze.' There were inconsistencies from witnesses surrounding the descriptions of vehicles used in the attacks and he said it was coincidental that the attacks took place near bus stops. There were many bus stops in west London and he claimed the trial could just as easily be referred to as 'the lamp-post case' as all the women would have been near lamp-posts when attacked, he said.

Mr Boyce said that Anna-Maria Rennie, who Bellfield allegedly attempted to abduct in Whitton in October 2001, was 'demonstrably unreliable' and urged the jury to assess her credibility in giving evidence. He referred to her admission that she may have drunk alcohol on the night of the incident and possibly used cannabis. 'Then you have someone who is not only half-baked but also taking drugs and drinking at the same time.' He reminded jurors that she admitted having no memory of the 10 to 20 minutes she spent talking to the man she said picked her up and dragged her towards his car before she escaped. Anna-Maria blamed her memory lapses on her dyslexia. 'This is only evidence in relation to the Anna-Maria case – there's no support for it at all. It's contradicted by other evidence – she contradicted herself. You have a witness who is demonstrably unreliable.' Police and forensic experts 'desperately squeezed' their findings to fit the profile of their target and the real culprit, he argued, was still on the loose.

Mr Boyce criticised the research gathered by police for their investigations into the murder of Marsha and into the attack on Irma Dragoshi. He told the court that the forensic imagery experts in charge of identifying the number plate on a car connected to Ms McDonnell's murder were 'self-taught and completely untrained'. Their enhancements and conclusions were too subjective and were tainted by 'confirmation bias' because they had been given a number plate to work towards by police, he added.

On Monday, 18 February, the jury retired to consider their verdict and returned their verdict the following Monday. Bellfield was the bus stop killer.

Levi Bellfield was found guilty of the murders of Amelie Delagrange and Marsha McDonnell and of the attempted murder of Kate Sheedy. The jury could not reach agreement on the charges relating to the other two women. The verdict was unanimous in the case of Amelie and by a 10–2 majority with Marsha and Kate. His reign of terror had at last come to an end, and the victims and their loved ones could, if not rejoice, then certainly take satisfaction from justice finally being done.

Marsha's uncle Shane said her parents Phil and Ute still found it too painful to talk about her death. 'On the day Marsha died, a part of Phil and Ute died with her. Marsha's murder was an act of pure evil, an innocent girl attacked from behind with no motive, no reason and no justification. Since the night five years ago when she was cruelly and unexpectedly taken away from this world, they as her family have had to endure a suffering that can only truly be known to those that have been through it. Losing a child in any circumstances is always an extremely hard loss to bear. To lose a child to such a barbaric act of violence that has no reason or explanation just compounds that grief further. The psychological and physical effects on us as a result of the manner of Marsha's death compromise their lives to this day.

'Marsha was a generous, loving, thoughtful girl. Her goodness, her sense of fun, her spirit and her zest for life are as fresh in our minds today as they were then. Marsha was enjoying a gap year after finishing school, deciding what career path to take. Like any teenager about to embark on the next stage of her life, she had many dreams and aspirations – which one man shattered. She was an artistic girl and her next step was to have fulfilled one of her passions by going to college to study photography. However, her other passion being music, there was a strong likelihood that she would have ended up following in her father's footsteps and embarked on a career working alongside him in his music industry business. Whatever Marsha chose to do, there is no doubt she would have achieved great success.'

He said her sisters and brother, Nathalie, Maya and Jack, would 'never know what it means to walk carefree down a street again. For the rest of their young lives this will remain a shadow over their happiness. One can only speculate on the damage this event has had on their education and careers. What is for certain, though, are the nightmares, the panic attacks, the hurt and sadness that is an ongoing fact of life for the three of them.

'On his way to the hospital the night of her attack, Phil had to pass the blood-soaked scene 60 yards from his home. The street where they have lived for over 20 years and raised all their children is forever tainted and every day provides a grim reminder of that fateful night. Despite this, the fact that the family home holds so many happy memories of Marsha means they could never consider moving. She was a person who truly made this world a better place for everyone – without her now our world is not complete any more. A missing colour in a rainbow. Only through our faith and the everlasting love for Marsha have we managed to stay a close family. The effects on our business were very serious and we almost became victims of losing our livelihoods as well. The pain and hurt that we as a family carry will be with us for life. It is a sentence that has no remission.'

Dominique Delagrange spoke of her loss. 'Our world fell apart on 19 August 2004. Amelie had a warm nature, she was lovely, she loved to laugh and joke. She was loving, always smiling and we could not be any closer. We laughed a lot together. I was proud of her, of her intention to travel alone like a mature adult. We did not want to let her go but it was not possible to stand in her way. It will always hurt us not to know what would have become of Amelie had her life not been severed in such a way. She wanted to marry, have children and her sister to be the godmother of her first child. So many unfulfilled hopes which are now intangible.

Alexis, her five-year-old godson, cries still today for his godmother who, as his parents told him, has become an angel for whom he sticks some drawings on the glass of his window so that she may see them from heaven.

'In fact, we are so reluctant to accept the death of Amelie that her grave is in reality a little garden always covered with flowers and grass. A stone will never be placed on it in the secret hope that Amelie will thus remain in our hearts the playful being, full of laughter, loved by her parents, relatives and friends, resting in the midst of crocuses that she so loved to pick in the spring. Her loss is an open wound that will never heal. We shall never get over it.'

Bellfield had appeared calm and respectful while the court was sitting. But that all changed when the jury members were not in their seats and trial judge Mrs Justice Rafferty was led out. He would turn to the relatives of his victims in the public gallery and wink or stare threateningly. Once he turned to Jean-Francois and Dominique Delagrange, and shouted, 'F★★★ off, leeches!' The couple later said that he had indulged in a 'remarkable level of arrogance' in court. Mrs Delagrange said she was horrified that he had been allowed to make rude gestures at her and shout obscenities. Mr Delagrange, who suffered a heart attack after losing his daughter, added, 'He thought he was above the law and would be found not guilty.'

Marsha's mother, Ute, said, 'I was annoyed at his monkey behaviour in court. It was particularly insulting to the

Delagrange family. It must be so much more difficult on top of the trauma.'

Kate Sheedy said, 'At times I could hear him laughing – it seemed wrong. When he smiled and laughed, he winked at my boyfriend Henry. It just made me feel sick.' Kate said she had suffered both physically and mentally since that night he attacked her with his vehicle. She said, 'I was in hospital. I was heavily sedated and was having horrible nightmares and hallucinations while I was awake. To this day I still suffer from nightmares. This is both reliving the incident itself and also the nightmares I had while I was in hospital. For a period of several months I suffered really bad panic attacks, flashbacks and nightmares. I couldn't be alone at all, even during the day. Even now I will not go out alone if it is dark, I'm too frightened to. If I'm out in the evening, even with lots of people, I dread the journey home because of what happened. Now I am able to get out alone if it is daylight but for the first few months I couldn't even do that. I then started seeing a counsellor. I saw the counsellor for a period of six weeks. I was then sent to West Middlesex hospital and tested for post-traumatic stress disorder [PTSD]. I was found to be suffering from PTSD and mild depression. I was told that it could take up to two years on the NHS to see a suitable counsellor so I ended up seeing a private counsellor. This started around the beginning of 2005. Although I still have some anxiety and nightmares, the counselling has greatly reduced these.

'While in hospital I had been unable to walk so I had to retrain my body to do all the things it should do and rebuild the strength in my muscles. I was still in a lot of pain. The sciatic nerve in my left leg had been badly bruised and this took a long time to fully recover. I still get pain in my right shoulder and down the back of my shoulder blade. This is especially so after repetitive arm movements, such as typing and if I've been carrying bags. I'm not able to play tennis or anything like that. Once when I went canoeing I was in a lot of pain and had to have several physio sessions. I still have a large visible scar on my lower back. The nerves in the area under the scar were completely severed and I have no feeling in the skin around this area. I suffered major muscle damage to my back and it took many months to rebuild these muscles and they are still not as strong as they were and may never get back to full strength. It still hurts to sit upright in a straight chair for any longer than an hour. This causes problems when I do things like going to the cinema. In the last 12 months I have needed four or five physio treatments. Since January 2005, I have had to pay for the physio as it has not been available to me on the NHS.'

Kate, who wept as the verdict was delivered, said she could not drive a car because she is 'only too aware of the power of the vehicle'. Outside court, she said, 'I have been waiting for nearly four years for this day and it's hard to express how much it means to me. At the time I was celebrating moving on to a new chapter of my life. All that hope and excitement was taken from me. The road to recovery has been long and hard and there have been times I thought I would not get better. I will never forget what happened to me. The fact that Bellfield has been found guilty means more to me than I can possibly say.' Meeting the families of Bellfield's murder victims had been 'a powerful reminder of what could have been. I hope that this verdict brings some comfort to all those families that have been affected by the despicable actions of just one man.'

Ray Wyre, a leading expert in the field of sexual criminology, said Bellfield's hatred of women indicated that he was motivated by anger against a main female figure in his life. 'He perceives women as demanding, hostile and unfaithful and uses this perception to justify his behaviour. The anger motive is tied in to the hammer attacks.'

Forensic psychologist Dr Keith Ashcroft said Bellfield's sinister obsession with similar-looking women revealed classic signs of the personality disorder erotomania. 'With this, the individual will relentlessly pursue the idea that their love object reciprocates romantic feelings or fantasies. In borderline erotomania, there is a meeting of violent tendencies, over-sensitivity to real or imagined rejection, intense depression and irrational fears of abandonment, which may have driven this person to kill.'

Bellfield had covered his tracks painstakingly. His swift attacks left no forensic details to trace. Except for the time he murdered Amelie, he always turned his telephone off so that its signal could never be traced to the scene. And the vehicles that linked him to crimes were sold or disposed of, sometimes never to be seen again. Three months into the Amelie investigation, police had identified a white Ford van parked at the Green at the time of the attack. But further enquiries led nowhere – the number plate could not be identified among the 26,000 vehicles of the same make registered in the UK. DCI Colin Sutton said, 'We just had to find this van. If necessary, we were going to have to visit 26,000 people.'

Meanwhile, officers went through 129 messages to the incident room from people claiming they knew someone who could be the killer. One caller was an ex-girlfriend, later identified as Johanna Collings. She said Bellfield was a wheel clamper with a white van and was violent. A detective remembered that a van owner in Isleworth had said he had sold his vehicle to a clamper and still had the mobile number of the purchaser. When the number was typed into a police computer, Bellfield's name came up as well as the information that he had reported neighbours as suspects to the national terrorism hotline. The people in question weren't terrorists but rather an innocent Italian family who Bellfield did not get on with. The mischievous phone call was one of Bellfield's few mistakes.

His van was discovered to have the same features – missing hubcap, missing left–hand front lamp and mark on the roof where an orange beacon had been removed – as that of the Ford on the CCTV. Police believed he propositioned Amelie Delagrange and killed her in a fit of rage when she showed no interest. CCTV images showed his white Ford Courier van and Amelie on foot.

Both slowed down as they approached the Green, appearing to fit with this theory. It was when police were certain they had enough evidence against him for Amelie's murder that they began to look at similar attacks in the past and discovered that he drove a white people carrier with distinctive blacked-out windows.

Yet there were errors in the original investigation of May 2004. CCTV footage of the van following the bus showed a petrol stain on the bodywork that matched a mark on Bellfield's vehicle. But officers looking at the images had got the wrong day. As a result, two officers were given written warnings and two were given verbal warnings after an Independent Police Complaints Commission (IPCC) investigation. It was a pre-trial inquiry carried out for the IPCC by the Metropolitan police's Directorate of Professional Standards and was a rap on the knuckles for the Met. But they had still gone on to get their man.

With the Bellfield–Sheedy link established, officers then looked into the unsolved murder of Marsha in February 2003. Again, there were no witnesses. Bellfield was ultra-careful in that respect. But CCTV footage from that night revealed a silver Vauxhall Corsa behaving oddly near Marsha's 111 bus. When she got off, the cameras showed, the car stopped and waited. The behaviour of the car driver was identical to that of the man behind the wheel of the people carrier. Bellfield had a silver Corsa registered to him and his clamping company which he later sold for £4,500 less than he paid for it.

The day after the jury's verdicts, the court was packed for the sentencing. There was only one person missing – Bellfield himself. The 20-stone brute refused to attend because of the 'bad publicity' he had received. Although defendants are not obliged to be in court during any criminal proceeding, his 'cowardice' was condemned by the families of his victims.

Mrs Justice Rafferty passed sentence as though Bellfield was in the dock, saying, 'You have reduced three families to unimagined grief. Marsha McDonnell was yards from her home in a quiet residential area of Hampton. Aged 19, she was beaten to the head and left to die on the pavement. Kate Sheedy lives due to her own courage and resource. The girl whom you left lying on the road after you had driven and then reversed over her said her goodbyes to her parents as she waited to die. Amelie Delagrange came to the UK expecting to be safe. She was beaten to the head and left to die on Twickenham Green. Three young women upon whom you preyed in the dark as they stood or walked near to or from buses. What dreadful feelings went through your head as you attacked and in two cases snuffed out a young life is beyond understanding.' She jailed Bellfield for life for each attack, saying, 'You will not be considered for parole and must serve your whole life in prison.'

The judge also addressed DCI Sutton and said the investigation had been a 'long road, sometimes rocky', adding, 'This case has depended on thousands of hours of unglamorous, painstaking work by officers who took their lead from you. One can imagine the collective will to do all that could be done for families devastated by grief and loss. Sweeping pronouncements do not bring a man to justice. Dedication and patience, determination and skill do – and yesterday it did.' There was a round of applause from other officers in the court as the judge told DCI Sutton, 'I commend you and your team.' Outside the court, he said, 'The fact that Bellfield did not come to court shows his cowardliness – the same cowardliness that he has shown throughout. He could not face the families, his victims and the judge and hear himself being sentenced.'

Jean-Francois Delagrange agreed outside court: 'It is just another show of his cowardice. He was a coward in his attacks and a coward today, the day he should pay for what he has done.'

Kate Sheedy added, 'I am disappointed that he wasn't here to hear the judge's words. I think that shows the kind of person he was – a complete coward. To know he is never going to see the light of day again is brilliant and a relief. Even if it were in 40 years' time, I would not have felt safe if he had been let out again.'

Colin Sutton said south-west London would be a safer place, especially for women, after Bellfield's conviction. 'He's a clever man, a cunning man, an arrogant man and obviously a very dangerous man. Throughout the last three and-a-half years he's lied, deceived people, tried to deceive people. He has never faced up to what he has done. He's tried to deflect the blame on others. Fortunately, the jury has seen through those lies and deceits and found him guilty of these serious offences. He had an interest in the opposite sex, an unhealthy interest. One of Levi's activities was to chat up women in the street in his car. There's a theory, and it's a reasonable one, that when they told him to go away he reacted badly to it.' Tellingly, DCI Sutton also added, 'We're now looking at a number of other offences, including murder, which he may be responsible for.'

The sentence meant Bellfield became the 37th prisoner for whom life would mean life. Many of those on the whole life tariff list had committed crimes so shocking their names lived on in the public consciousness for decades. They included Moors murderer Ian Brady, who tortured and murdered children with Myra Hindley, and murderer and robber Donald Neilson. Known as the Black Panther, Neilson shot and killed three sub-postmasters, and he also abducted and killed heiress Lesley Whittle, 17, whose body was found at the bottom of a drain shaft. The only woman on the list was Rose West, convicted in 1995. A killing spree with husband Fred saw ten young women murdered, including her own daughter Heather, 16, and step-daughter Charmaine, eight. Jeremy Bamber was also serving life after being convicted of murdering five members of his adoptive family, a crime he had always denied. Civil servant Dennis Nilsen received a whole-life sentence after he strangled six young men then dismembered and burned their bodies. In 2005, Glyn Dix was convicted of stabbing his wife Hazel to death and chopping her body into 16 pieces using a knife, hacksaw and scissors. Dix, who had already served a life sentence for a previous murder, butchered his wife in the kitchen of the couple's home in Redditch. Mrs Dix's son came

But in an interview with the *Daily Mirror*, conducted from Wakefield prison in April 2009, he admitted driving the red car. 'It doesn't take a lot to work out, does it?' he said. 'Coming down a road where you live, it's hardly breaking the law. There's not many red Daewoos floating about in Walton-on-Thames, so we've got to be realistic about it. But then I've got to be careful about how I answer these questions. I did use the Daewoo once and I was stopped by the police once in it for speeding.'

He was asked about the way the rear of the vehicle was near the ground, as if it had a load in the boot. Bellfield said a 'human body' would not have been heavy enough to make the vehicle sit that close to the ground. 'If you look at that imagery of that vehicle pulling out, it's very low to the ground isn't it? It's practically on the floor. Now, I say it's on the floor because it's loaded up with tiles I was buying in Shepperton at the time, yeah? They were to tile the kitchen. I also believe if it's possible it [CCTV image] should be enhanced and you'll see the back seats are actually down. Are you with me? Well, any human being wouldn't put it that low.'

A police spokesman said, 'Operation Ruby, the Surrey police investigation into Milly Dowler's murder, is a vigorous and live inquiry and we remain determined to find Milly's killer. Speculation can be unhelpful and potentially hurtful to Milly's family but we will thoroughly investigate any new lines of inquiry. In the 12 months following our renewed appeal in February 2008, Surrey police received more than 300 calls from members of the public. We would still urge anyone with information about Milly's murder to make contact with us if they have not yet done so.'

By August 2009, a dossier naming Bellfield as Milly's killer was being prepared for prosecutors with what was described as 'compelling fresh evidence'. Surrey police filled five files with a huge amount of circumstantial evidence linking him to the crime. Sources close to the inquiry said the new evidence emerged the previous December. Officials at the Crown Prosecution Service (CPS) would use the information to gauge whether or not there was a realistic prospect of obtaining a conviction.

On 30 March 2010 came the news that everyone had been waiting for. 'After carefully reviewing all the evidence in this case, I have now reached the decision that there is sufficient evidence and that it is in the public interest to charge Levi Bellfield with three offences,' said CPS lawyer Nigel Pilkington. 'Accordingly, summonses have been obtained from Staines magistrates' court and will now be served.' Mr Pilkington said he would be meeting Milly's parents to explain the reasoning.

Bellfield was also charged with the attempted kidnap of a 12-year-old girl on 20 March 2002, the day before Milly disappeared. Police said a man matching Bellfield's description and driving a red Daewoo Nexia approached Rachel Cowles in Shepperton, a few miles from where Milly was abducted. Mr Pilkington added, 'While the considerable media interest in this case is known and is understood, I would remind all concerned that Levi Bellfield now stands charged with criminal offences and that he has a right to a fair trial.'

DCI Woodall said, 'Milly's family have been kept informed of all the developments and our thoughts remain with Milly's family today. This continues to be an extremely difficult and traumatic time for them.'

On 13 April, Bellfield appeared by video link from Wakefield prison at Staines magistrates' court in south-west London. He was remanded in custody at the end of a brief hearing and ordered to attend Guildford crown court on 30 April. Wearing a blue polo shirt with a bright-red logo, his hair close-shaven, Bellfield took notes throughout the hearing, as was his habit in court appearances. He spoke only to confirm his date of birth and to say he could see and hear clearly and understood what took place as the clerk of the court read the charges against him. At the end of April, Bellfield appeared at Guildford, again by video, to face the charges against him relating to Milly and Rachel Cowles. Clean-shaven and wearing a navy-blue sweater he spoke only to answer to his name as the case was sent to the Old Bailey for trial. On 6 October, he appeared at the Bailey, again via video, when the trial was set for May 2011.

It was to be one of the most sensational trials in modern British legal history, not just for the dramatic evidence that was to be revealed, but for the controversy that it caused both within the legal system and in the country at large.

CHAPTER 9

The second Old Bailey trial of Levi Bellfield began in court number eight on 10 May 2011. The public gallery was crowded and the demand from the media was so great that tickets were allocated in advance. Bellfield was again being prosecuted by the formidable Brian Altman, now a Queen's Counsel and chief prosecutor at the court.

Milly's disappearance and the discovery of her body had shocked the nation. Now Mr Altman was to describe the events with more detail than had previously been heard in public. He was also to set out the case of Rachel Cowles who, Mr Altman said, Bellfield tried to kidnap the day before Milly's disappearance.

Smartly dressed Bellfield sauntered into the dock, hand in pocket, to deny the charges of murder and kidnapping of Milly and the attempted kidnapping of 12-year-old Rachel. His attitude that opening day set the tone for his behaviour throughout the trial. At times, he listened keenly and passed notes to his legal advisers through the thick window screen around the dock. At other points, he was bored and indifferent, as though he was doing the world a favour by attending court. He had, his body language seemed to imply, more important things to attend to.

It took more than a day for Mr Altman to set out the case against Bellfield. As in the first trial, some of the information was already known, but much of it was not. It was both engrossing and chilling as he uncovered layer by layer, like some rotten onion, the life and deeds of Levi Bellfield. There is not space to record verbatim Mr Altman's lengthy opening to the jury of seven men and five women. Yet his remarks were transmitted around the world that day and there was great public interest in the case of poor Milly. Therefore, his words do merit recording in some detail. (Though passages containing telephone numbers, car registrations and unnecessary information have been deleted.)

Mr Altman, a tall, bespectacled figure, told the hushed courtroom: 'Just over nine years ago now, on Thursday, 21 March 2002, 13-year-old Amanda Dowler – or Milly, as she preferred to be known – had spent an ordinary day at school in Weybridge, Surrey. At the end of the school day Milly, who was in her school uniform, took the train with friends from Weybridge station to Walton-on-Thames station. There she alighted on to the platform with her friends and spent a little time with them at the station cafe, eating chips, before leaving to make her way home on foot along Station Avenue to her home in Walton-on-Thames, no more than a mile away. Within moments of leaving the station to walk along the road, just a few minutes after 4.00pm, she vanished, gone in the blink of an eye.

'On any other school day she would have simply continued her journey home on the train from Weybridge to Hersham station, which was closer to her house. But on this day an entirely innocent and quite ordinary diversion to a station cafe to buy some chips with some school friends was a decision that was to cost Milly her life because it meant her taking a fateful journey along Station Avenue where, unbeknown to her, her abductor and killer was soon to strike.

'Milly had simply disappeared in a flash from a street in a suburban town in broad daylight. Her sudden and unexplained disappearance that March afternoon set in train what was to become a massive missing person's enquiry and a police investigation on a national scale. This was, of course, every parent's worst nightmare. For six long months the Dowler family suffered the excruciating agony of not knowing what had become of their daughter – until Wednesday, 18 September 2002. Some mushroom pickers found, quite by chance, the unclothed and badly decomposed body of a young female, some 25 miles away from where she had last been seen alive on Station Avenue, Walton, lying in the undergrowth of Yateley Heath Woods in Hampshire. The body was soon identified as that of Milly Dowler. The decomposition of her body was such that the cause of her death could not be ascertained. The prosecution's case is that the person who abducted and killed Milly Dowler was this defendant, Levi Bellfield.

'At this time, Bellfield, together with his partner, Emma Mills, their two children and a Staffordshire bull terrier dog, occupied a rented ground-floor flat at 24 Collingwood Place in Walton. The flat at Collingwood Place in Walton was literally just yards away from the spot where Milly was last seen alive in Station Avenue. However, during the period covering Milly's abduction and murder, the defendant and his family were not living at Collingwood Place, Walton, because they were house-sitting for a friend who was away on holiday in West Drayton, Middlesex, which was little more than half a mile away from their own family home at Little Benty, also in West Drayton, where the defendant and his family had not lived for some time for reasons to which I shall come.

'Although Emma Mills and her children were not at the flat at 24 Collingwood Place over the period we are dealing with in March 2002, the prosecution say there is evidence that this defendant was at or in the vicinity of the flat on Thursday, 21 March 2002. Because, within around 22 minutes of what the prosecution say was Milly's abduction by him from Station Avenue, a red Daewoo Nexia car, which the defendant was using at this time, was captured by CCTV leaving the area by the access road to the flats and then driving away in Station Avenue.'

Mr Altman then went on to describe the charge involving

Rachel Cowles, the first time the world had heard of what, the prosecution said, was Bellfield's attempt to kidnap her. 'But Thursday, 21 March 2002 was not the only day over this period the defendant was in Walton. There is evidence that he was there the previous day, Wednesday, 20 March 2002, also. On that Wednesday, at around the same time that Milly was to be abducted the very next day, there was an attempt to abduct another schoolgirl, who was walking home from school along Upper Halliford Road in Shepperton, a mere nine-minute and 3.3-mile car journey north of Walton.

'Rachel Cowles, almost 12 at the time, was approached by a man in a small red car, driven, say the prosecution, by a man resembling the defendant, who tried tricking her by telling her that he had just moved in next door and he asked her if she wanted a lift. Sensibly she did not accept his offer. At this time, a police car was driving along the road, which possibly spooked the man, and he drove off. Years later, Rachel attended an identification parade but she failed to identify the defendant as the man.

'The prosecution say there can be no doubt that Levi Bellfield, and no one else, was responsible for both. He has been proven to be a predatory and violent offender towards young women, with convictions in 2008 at this very court for the murders and the attempted murder of three young women in west London: Marsha McDonnell in February 2003, Kate Sheedy in May 2004 and then Amelie Delagrange in August 2004. So all committed by him within a period of just over two years from the abduction of Rachel Cowles and the abduction and murder of Milly Dowler in March 2002. I shall have more to say about the detail of those convictions later. It is also open to you to use the evidence of one as informing your view about the other and vice versa. This is because, when you come to analyse the evidence in relation to the offences, not only is there evidence suggesting that the defendant is guilty of the offences, but also there are, we say, such similarities between the offences that the chances of them having been committed by two or more men working independently of each other can safely and sensibly be excluded. Such that the offences you may conclude were the work of one man and that that man was this defendant, Levi Bellfield.

Referring to the crimes for which Bellfield had already been convicted, Altman said, 'The prosecution say that the commission by him of those offences, albeit committed after the abduction of Rachel Cowles and the abduction and killing of Milly Dowler the very next day, makes it more likely that he is the man who committed those offences also. After all, you may wish to consider how likely it is that there were two such people, disposed to behave in exactly the same way, in the same place at the very same time. So the prosecution say that out of an extremely limited number of people with the opportunity and indeed capacity to have committed such serious offences, he alone was likely to have done so.

'Having said that, the prosecution are not inviting you to

convict him of these offences simply because he was convicted of other serious offences in 2008, but we do say that they, together with the rest of the evidence you are to hear, provide a compelling picture that he and he alone committed them. The prosecution say that, when you examine the direct and the circumstantial evidence in the case of these offences, the chances that these offences were committed by anyone other than Levi Bellfield are so fanciful that you may reject them.'

Mr Altman was crystal clear in his delivery. He next turned to the victims and the man he said had committed offences against them. Milly, he said, was born on 25 June 1988 and, had she lived, she would have been 23 next month. 'Milly was slim, pretty and intelligent but she was not confident, according to her mother and needed encouragement to participate in activity. She was popular among her friends. She was attaining the usual milestones to be expected of a young teenager. To all intents and purposes she was an ordinary girl who was developing into a fine young woman.

'Rachel Cowles was born on 4 April 1990. On 20 March 2002, she was two weeks shy of her 12th birthday. She is now 21 years of age. At the time she was a schoolgirl at Bishop Wand Church of England School in Laytons Lane, Sunbury, a few miles north of Walton. She lived with her family in Shepperton. Levi Bellfield was born on 17 May 1968 in Isleworth and so he is now 43 years old. He has worked as a doorman and in more recent times ran a clamping business. He has lived and worked in west and south-west London most, if not all, of his life and knows that area, as well as Walton and Shepperton, extremely well. He is left-handed, around 6 foot 1 inch in height and is big built. He is commonly known as "Lee".

'His partner during the time period we are dealing with was Emma Mills whom he had met in 1995–1996 when he was working as a doorman at Rocky's nightclub in Cobham. She is an important witness in the case, and what I am going to do is to start by telling you about her and Collingwood Place, as well as provide you with the detail of other important background evidence, all of which is going to help you understand the case.'

He told the jury how Emma was 18 or 19 when she first met Bellfield while she was still living at home with her mother Gillian in Hersham. As the relationship developed, they moved in with Bellfield's uncle, Charlie Brazil, in Walton. Later they moved to a bed-sitting room in Twickenham, not very far from the location of the defendant's 2004 murder of Amelie Delagrange on Twickenham Green. In late 1997, while she was pregnant with the first of their children, Emma obtained a council flat in Hounslow where she lived with the defendant. In December 1997, the first of their children – a girl – was born and in October 1999 the second of their three children together – a boy – was born. The third child was not born until July 2004, long after the immediate events we are dealing with.

'Later, still, in about 2000, they exchanged the Hounslow flat for one at Little Benty, West Drayton, Middlesex, which was to become the family home. However, the relationship broke down and about August 2001 Emma left the defendant and moved out of Little Benty with the children and went to live in a women's refuge. Because the refuge proved unsuitable, Gillian Mills, Emma's mother, arranged the rental of an unfurnished flat for Emma and the children. This flat was at 24 Collingwood Place in Walton-on-Thames. While Emma and the children were living at 24 Collingwood Place, initially the defendant remained living at Little Benty. However, Emma was soon to resume her relationship with him and, according to Emma, some six weeks after she had moved in, the defendant began living with her at 24 Collingwood Place.'

He said that Mills moved in, according to letting and management agency Jackson's, on 21 September 2001. Jackson's had a record of a one-year lease on the two-bedroom flat with a six-month break clause. She gave notice to quit on 1 March 2002, which meant she could vacate around the end of April or beginning of May 2002. 'It was the abduction and murder on the afternoon of Thursday, 21 March 2002 that we suggest was to change all that. And the defendant, Emma and his family suddenly moved from 24 Collingwood Place back to their relatively uninhabitable family home at Little Benty in West Drayton. However, it had not been Emma's desire or intention to move at that time or with such indecent haste. That decision, like all decisions, had been Bellfield's – a decision to begin the process of moving out of 24 Collingwood Place and back to Little Benty the day following those terrible events in Walton.'

Mr Altman then turned his attention the £800 Daewoo Nexia which Mills' mother bought for her when she moved into Collingwood Place and which Bellfield regularly drove. 'According to Emma, fixed to the back seat of the car was an old-fashioned Britax child seat which was grey in colour and quite chunky, as she puts it. Emma says she felt sure there was only the one proper child car seat. But she thinks there was in the car also a booster seat for the older child to give her more height, which was black-and-pink or grey-and-pink in colour. The car was in reasonable condition but the interior was often untidy, with magazines and other rubbish inside it. The wheels had plain silver hubcaps but, as Emma recalls it, one of the front hubcaps had come off so that the wheel looked black.

'The red Daewoo Nexia owned by Emma but driven by Bellfield over the critical days in March 2002 was on 29 March 2002 reported as having been stolen on, or about, 26 March 2002, within days of Milly going missing. Despite a vast police hunt for it, that car has never been found. You will see that one feature of the defendant's behaviour following certainly two of the offences for which the defendant was convicted in 2008 was that afterwards he disposed of the cars he was using at the time of the commission of the offences. Before and at the time of Amelie Delagrange's murder in August 2004, the defendant had been driving a white Ford Courier van, which he owned. That van simply disappeared, and, despite a massive police search, was also never found. The vehicles the defendant used to offend provided him, of course, with the means by which he would target his victims and then flee the scene. The white Ford Courier van in August 2004, like the red Daewoo Nexia before it in March 2002, he knew, linked him with the offences and so their complete and permanent disposal was one of the means, but not the only means, by which he put as much distance as he could between what he had done and himself. Moving away, or taking a sudden holiday, was another, as we shall see.

'There was, however, one difference between his approach to those other offences and the abduction and murder of Milly. In her case he did not have the need to use a car to spot her because he was, we say, at the flat at Collingwood Place that afternoon and she just happened to pass by his doorstep. But the defendant still had to make the red Daewoo Nexia disappear for reasons I shall return to.'

Mr Altman said that between 20 and 21 March 2002, Emma Mills was not staying at 24 Collingwood Place but was house-sitting for her friend, Christine Hawgood – who was also known as Richardson. Her address was 14 Harmondsworth Road, West Drayton, very close to the Bellfield family home at 11 Little Benty. No one was sleeping at Collingwood Place. 'As I say, the defendant was also staying overnight with Emma at Christine Hawgood's home. But it is perfectly clear that he was at Collingwood Place in Walton on both Wednesday, 20 March and Thursday, 21 March 2002, when clearly he would have had the run of the flat – completely undisturbed, to himself – because

CCTV captured a red Daewoo Nexia, consistent with it being Emma's Daewoo Nexia, emerging from Copenhagen Way, an access road to the flats, and driving into Station Avenue on both those days. The prosecution say it was the defendant driving it.

'But that is not all. Contacts to and from his mobile phone indicated that that phone, and therefore Bellfield, in whose possession we say that phone was, was at or in the vicinity of the flat at Collingwood Place on the early afternoon of Wednesday, 20 March and indeed the morning, afternoon and evening of Friday, 22 March 2002, the day after the abduction of Milly Dowler from Station Avenue.'

Mr Altman then turned to the Rachel Cowles incident. 'A man in a car had tried to engage Rachel on the very day before she recalled hearing the news about Milly Dowler's disappearance. That day was Wednesday, 20 March 2002. It had been an ordinary school day for Rachel, which ended at 3.15pm. Rachel walked home alone dressed in her school uniform, which was a grey skirt, white blouse and navy blazer, bearing a school badge on the left breast pocket. She had on her school tie. She wore black shoes and flesh-coloured tights. She remembered carrying her blue-shaded, mono-strap rucksack. Her hair was up in a ponytail, as was Milly's hair the following day.' Mr Altman said she bore 'an uncanny resemblance to how Milly looked when she left school the following day'. Rachel was in Upper Halliford Road, Shepperton, sometime between 3.30pm and 3.45pm when 'suddenly a red car pulled up next to where she was walking and it stopped, although the engine remained on. She did not recall seeing the car turn but Rachel believed that the car had come from the opposite direction, i.e. from the direction of Walton, but had turned around before pulling up and stopping behind her, so that the passenger side was kerbside. From what Rachel remembered of it, the car was red, but not bright red or dark red. It was not metallic. The car had five doors. It was bigger than a Fiesta but smaller than a Rover 214 which her parents had at that time.'

'She recalled there being magazines on the floor at the back of the car. As she remembered it, there were two baby seats in the back of the car. Both she thought were patterned, but one seemed green-blue in colour – or possibly a dark shade of blue – and the one she thought she saw on the passenger side of the car, nearest the kerb by which the car stopped, was pink. Because of the colours she remembered thinking that one was for a boy and the other for a girl but not for newborn children. When asked on a later occasion to see if she could say any more about the car seats, she thought they were probably for a child coming up to one or more.'

'Rachel recalled that the driver of the car was white, aged, Rachel thought, in his thirties to forties. In March 2002, the defendant was 33. As Rachel recalled it, the man appeared to be bald and he had a chubby head – which she described as "sort of round and large". He had a gold earring in his left ear which she believed to be a hoop. According to Emma Mills, at the time the defendant would often wear gold, hooped earrings in his ears. So all these descriptive features are capable of fitting the defendant at that time. When the car stopped, the passenger window was wound down. The driver leant over and said to Rachel something along the lines of, "Hello, I've just moved in next door. Would you like a lift?"

'Rachel's sensible reaction was to refuse. Instinctively, she thought something was not right and within moments she saw a police car travelling towards them on the opposite side of the road and the man drove off in the direction of Walton. He had probably stopped for a minute or so in total, Rachel thought. This, say the prosecution, was an attempted abduction because the driver – Bellfield, say the prosecution – had sought to deceive Rachel into taking a lift by saying he was her new neighbour when clearly he was not. He had done all he needed to do to get Rachel into his car which makes it an attempt in law. Had she not seen through the trick and taken him up on his offer that would have amounted to the full offence of kidnapping – abduction – whether or not he had then gone on to use force to complete the offence. But the consequences would have been the same – for then Rachel would have been under his control and entirely at his mercy.'

The QC began to describe the background to CCTV images that were taken in the area. 'There were two cameras operating on the outside of the Birds Eye building in 2002 – camera one at the eastern end of the building, effectively opposite Trafalgar Drive on the north side of Station Avenue and camera two at the western end, effectively opposite Copenhagen Way. Footage recorded by camera two will occupy us the most … The cameras were dome-type CCTV cameras which rotated anti-clockwise through 360 degrees, making one complete rotation every 42 seconds. And they were operational only during certain hours of the day – they ceased recording between 9.00pm and 6.00am. The view afforded by them included views along both sides of Station Avenue, down towards Walton railway station itself in the distance to the west and towards what is known locally as The Halfway at the eastern end of Station Avenue.'

He noted that sunlight and rain had affected the quality of the images: 'When the CCTV footage was examined, police discovered that camera two had captured a red hatchback car leaving Copenhagen Way, and turning left into Station Avenue. The red car we see leaving the estate by that road was, says the imagery expert Andrew Laws, a Daewoo Nexia. The reason, of course, that he could not compare the images of the departing car against the Daewoo Nexia Emma owned and the defendant used is because it disappeared within days of these events and has never been recovered. The police team investigating the case made a timed run from where the red car is seen tuning into Station Avenue to Upper Halliford Road, in Shepperton, where Rachel was stopped. The journey time, conforming to traffic signals and speed limits en route, was nine minutes and the distance 3.3 miles. So the car we can see leaving Copenhagen Way [at 3.26pm] could very easily have been in Upper Halliford Road by 3.35pm –

which is the very time frame in which Rachel was accosted by the man in the red car.

'The prosecution say that that red Daewoo Nexia was Emma's car but it was being driven by the defendant, as he left [the Collingwood Place estate] to drive into Station Avenue.' Mr Altman said the prosecution case was supported by phone records, analysed by an expert, which showed where and when Bellfield's mobile was switched on and off. 'We will see the identical thing occurring on the day that Milly went missing, on Thursday, 21 March 2002. As for Rachel, when she got outside her house she looked out for the man's car to see if he was indeed her new neighbour. There was, of course, no such car and as soon as she got indoors she told her mother what had happened. Her mother Diane telephoned the police and the record of that call shows the call was made at 4.03pm on Wednesday, 20 March 2002. Rachel, who went on the telephone briefly during the call to speak to the emergency operator, was too distressed by what had happened to give any useful information at that time. Diane Cowles did not recall any near neighbour owning a red car. It is clear that the man had deliberately lied to Rachel – you may think for one purpose only, which was to entice her by deceit and/or eventually by force into his car.

'On 22 May 2005, over three years after the incident, Rachel was asked to attend a video identification procedure at which the defendant was paraded together with eight other volunteers.

Rachel failed to make any identification at all. She picked out no one.'

Mr Altman then described the last day that Milly was seen alive. 'On 21 March, Sally had a tutorial lesson at the end of the day, Gemma had PE practice and Milly had some artwork to complete after school and so the initial arrangement had been for Sally to take both girls home by car. At 2.55pm at the end of the school day, however, Milly went to her mother's office where she told her mother that she had completed her artwork during her lunch break and so she was going to get the train home instead of waiting for her mother to give her a lift home. To her mother, Milly seemed absolutely fine and she was acting no differently to any other school day. Milly's father, Robert, or Bob, Dowler, worked in London for an IT recruitment consultancy. Because of this, Milly would ordinarily return home to an empty house. Unusually, on Thursday, 21 March Robert Dowler had a meeting in Basingstoke and left for his meeting from home instead of going into London. He was home by 3.10pm. At the time of these events, the Dowlers were having an extension built and builders had been in the house but they had departed by 3.10pm.

'CCTV footage at Heathside School captured Milly walking through and out of the school at 3.07pm. From there she walked to Weybridge station where CCTV … captured her walking through the station. Both CCTV systems help show what Milly was wearing at the time she was captured, and what she was carrying. The school footage shows Milly wearing her school uniform, consisting of a short grey skirt – worn above the knee – white blouse, light-blue, V-neck jumper and navy-blue blazer with an emblem over the left breast pocket. The tie she was wearing cannot be seen beneath the sweater she is wearing. Her school shoes were black Pod shoes. She was wearing white trainer socks but otherwise no tights. According to her mother, she was probably wearing a set of small gold earrings – studs or hoops – a silver band ring with a turquoise stone inset into it and a small, pink, beaded friendship bracelet. Her friend Danielle Sykes confirms that she was wearing her friendship bracelet. Her mother thinks Milly's blazer might have had pinned to it stud earrings in the shape of crucifixes.

'The school CCTV footage clearly shows that Milly's hair was tied back into a ponytail. As I have pointed out, all this bearing striking similarity to how Rachel had looked the previous day. On her back, Milly can be seen to be carrying what her mother says was a beige and black JanSport rucksack. Its contents would have included her schoolbooks, a glittery pencil case – according to Gemma this was a pink Barbie pencil case – and a red and white purse bearing heart shapes. She also had with her a Nokia 3210 mobile phone with her name marked on it and her house keys on a distinctive bottle-opener-style key ring. Not one of these items has ever been recovered.'

Mr Altman said that Milly left school with Danielle Sykes, Cara Dawson and Jacqueline Pignolly and the train they boarded at Weybridge arrived at Walton shortly afterwards. 'Ordinarily, Milly would have continued her journey to the next train stop at Hersham station, closer to home, where she would have alighted. However, breaking from her usual routine, on this day she was persuaded by Danielle Sykes to leave the train at Walton station to buy some chips at the station cafe, the Travellers Cafe, located on the station platform. Jacqueline continued on the train to Hersham and Cara left Milly and Danielle at Walton station and went home – along Station Avenue, across the junction, the Halfway and into Rydens Road. That was the route Milly should have walked home, but, unlike Cara, Milly never made it.

'So it was that Milly and Danielle went to the cafe where Danielle lent Amanda 10p for some chips. There they sat down and chatted. Inside the café were fellow Heathside students who had been on the same train. They were: Christopher Price, Adam Raine and Miles Pink. Although Milly had her own mobile phone with her, she had no credit and so at one point she asked Christopher Price if she could borrow his mobile phone to call her father. He lent her the phone and she called her father. Milly spoke to him, telling him she would be a little late home. Robert Dowler recalls Milly's call being at 3.45pm. She told him that she was at Walton station cafe having some chips with Danielle and that she would be home in around 30 minutes. According to her father, she sounded fine. Christopher Price's mobile phone records show that Milly made the call using his phone at 3.47pm and the call lasted 26 seconds. So Milly must have expected to be home very roughly by about 4.20pm.

'Danielle's sister, 17-year-old Natalie Sykes, who was studying at Esher college, called Danielle and asked her to wait for her because she was travelling from Esher station to Walton station … She estimated that she would have been in the cafe at some time before 4.00pm. She recalls that it was when she got there that Milly ordered her chips, which came within about five minutes. Danielle thought that she and her sister left the station somewhere between 4.00pm and 4.05pm. Natalie thought it might have been between 4.10pm and 4.15pm that they left. As Milly got up to leave, Danielle asked her if she was all right to walk home alone. She said she was fine. This exchange makes it clear, you may think, that Milly's intention was to walk home from the station, a journey of about a quarter of an hour and a direct route – down Station Avenue, across the Halfway, into Rydens Road and then right into Walton Park.

'To walk home, Danielle and her sister Natalie walked down the steps of the main entrance to the station and went left past the taxi rank and into the subway tunnel which runs under the railway tracks. They last saw Milly as she was at the gate at the end of the platform, which at that time led to an exit slope past the eastern end of the station building, past some advertising hoardings and directly into Station Avenue. Anthony Stevens, the owner of the station cafe at the time, recalls the group inside the cafe. Stevens believes that when he saw Milly in the cafe getting up to leave she had her blazer over her arm and her hair was tied back into a ponytail, as it had been earlier. Christopher Price, who had lent her his phone, recalled her having her blazer off in the cafe. Natalie Sykes, however, thought she was wearing her blazer when she last saw her at the gate at the end of the platform. The next and last witness to see her, Katherine Laynes, saw her without her blazer on. I shall come to Katherine Laynes in a moment.

'Anthony Stevens had a brief sighting of Milly from one of the cafe windows, turning right out of the station area along Station Avenue at what he estimated to be around 4.15pm. He last saw her on the pavement outside the station. At the same time he saw the Sykes sisters walking away from the station in the opposite direction clearly, before entering the subway on their way home. Although this was broad daylight and the end of a school day, when you might expect a road like Station Avenue to be busy, when we come to look at the CCTV footage from the Birds Eye building of the critical period in time when Milly went missing you will find it remarkable how relatively quiet Station Avenue really was at the time. When I say Station Avenue was relatively quiet at that time, what I mean is that there were very few people about and few cars driving up and down the road. We will also see that there was a line of cars parked along the south side of Station Avenue in the marked bays.

'The last known person to have seen Milly alive is Katherine Laynes, who I have already mentioned in passing. She was a year-11 girl at Heathside School, aged 15 at the time. She was friendly with Milly's older sister, Gemma, and she knew Milly.' Mr Altman said the schoolgirl arrived at Walton station at about 4.03pm and sat at the bus stop on the north side of Station Avenue. She thought she was at the stop for about ten minutes when she saw Milly Dowler walking along Station Avenue on the opposite side of the road in the direction of the Halfway. According to Katherine, they made eye contact ... When Katherine saw her, Milly was alone. Milly walked to Katherine's left, crossing the entrance to the station car park, but Katherine lost sight of her when the advertising board side of the bus shelter obscured her vision.

'Katherine recalls boarding the bus on her own. She went to the left-hand side and sat around two to three rows back from the front at a window seat. She thinks she was the only person on the bus. The bus ticketing information suggests that she is right. Katherine was sitting with her back against the window looking across the bus and out through the window on the other side. As the bus moved off, she expected to see Milly again in Station Avenue, given the time difference between her last seeing her and the bus arriving and so she looked out for her on the same side she had seen her walking. But she failed to see her. She did not look for her on the left side of the road as there was no reason she could see for Milly to cross over. The bus had to stop at the Halfway traffic lights before turning left. As it did so, Katherine looked down Rydens Road but did not see Milly there either.'

Andrew Laws had gone over footage from the Birds Eye building, Mr Altman said, from 4.00pm to 4.50pm that day. 'This exercise involved the imagery expert examining every sighting of every individual walking on either side of Station Avenue during the period to exclude that person as being Milly. He also examined the possibility of any vehicles arriving or leaving from the area between Copenhagen Way and the bike shelter on Station Avenue or vehicles passing between Copenhagen Way and the station in the same time period stopping. His conclusions were that none of the sightings corresponded with the appearance of Milly Dowler on that day. He found that it was not possible for Milly to have passed along Station Avenue on the south side without being captured by the CCTV system on the Birds Eye building and indeed she is not captured passing it. He added that it was possible Milly could have reached as far as the vicinity of the station car park entrance on the south side of Station Avenue, i.e. where Katherine Laynes last saw her, but no further. He found that it was not possible for her to have walked down Station Avenue on the north side past Copenhagen Way without being detected or imaged.

'If you conclude, as we say you can, that Milly did not walk past the Birds Eye building in Station Avenue, then she must have diverted or been diverted from her route home. And if she did not walk past the Birds Eye building, then not only was Katherine Laynes the last known person to have seen Milly alive but also Milly disappeared soon after that sighting. If that evidence is accurate and reliable, then it means that Milly had to have been taken from that part of Station Avenue right outside Collingwood Place and right on the defendant's doorstep.

'Sally and Gemma Dowler arrived home from school by about 4.45pm. When it became clear that Milly had gone missing, the Dowlers and others searched for Milly. Needless to say, she was not to be found. There was simply no trace of her and at 7.07pm that evening Robert Dowler reported his daughter missing to Addlestone police station. There then began one of the largest and longest missing person's inquiries this country has ever seen.'

Mr Altman said that Andrew Laws had also examined CCTV footage from the Birds Eye building of red cars in the Station Avenue area on 20 and 21 March. He said there was 'strong support' for the contention that one captured on camera within 22 minutes of Katherine Laynes buying her ticket was a Daewoo Nexia. Mr Altman also referred to Bellfield's phone being switched off and said that, on 21 March, 'from 3.28pm onwards that day his mobile phone was unreachable, with calls being diverted to voicemail – we suggest deliberately switched off – until 4.48pm, when he rang his mother from the area of Hanworth where she lived'. The prosecutor noted there were other silent times. 'The fact his phone was unreachable during these periods is, you may think, not so much some remarkable coincidence but a deliberate ploy by him when out committing offences, just as it had been on the previous day also when – the prosecution say – he tried to lure Rachel Cowles into his car and his phone was unreachable – we suggest switched off – from 1.51pm to 9.12pm.'

Mr Altman referred to the previous trial where Bellfield's phone had been off around the times of the attacks on Amelie Delagrange and Kate Sheedy. 'As I have suggested, turning his phone off served two purposes. It permitted him to offend in this way without unwelcome disturbance from Emma Mills, and Bellfield – whom we suggest is and was forensically aware – well knew that it ensured that anyone looking at his phone records could not site his phone at the actual time he was offending.'

Mr Altman then turned to Bellfield's movements the day Milly vanished. 'According to Emma Mills, on the Thursday, the defendant just disappeared during the day and this was, she says, unusual. She had been trying to ring him all day from Christine Hawgood's house but without success. It is clear why. He had deliberately switched the phone off. On a normal day they would speak a number of times. However, he was not working during that period – at least not in the daytime, as would require him to have his phone off. She recalled possibly speaking to him later before he arrived home. Indeed, it is clear from his phone records that he called the Hawgood landline, but not until 5.38pm.

'Emma did not see him, she estimates, until between about 10.30pm and 11.00pm when he returned to Christine Hawgood's house. Emma noticed immediately that he had changed his clothing, which made her think that he must have returned to Collingwood Place because that is where he had his clothes. There was nothing at Little Benty because at that time the house was uninhabitable. She could tell he had had a drink but he was not drunk. If Emma is right that he had changed his clothing by the time of his return to Little Benty that night, then her evidence serves to confirm the significant fact that not only had the defendant been to Walton-on-Thames that day but that he must also have been inside the flat in order to change his clothing. Emma was suspicious that the defendant had been with another woman. She knew he had the keys to the flat as they were on the car key fob and he had the car. But she did not ask him where he had been.

'About 3–4 in the morning on Friday, 22 March, when Emma was in bed with the defendant, she awoke to find him suddenly getting dressed. She asked him what he was doing. He answered, "I'm going to go back to the flat, 'cause I'm going to have a lay-in." The flat to which he was referring returning to was, of course, 24 Collingwood Place, where he had been earlier that day. You will want to ask yourselves what was it that was so important that in the middle of the night he decided to get up and drive over to Walton – a trip which a timed run demonstrated took just over 27 minutes at that time in the morning and covered a distance of some 13.7 miles. You can be sure that it was no "lie-in".'

Mr Altman said that, in the early hours of Friday, 22 March, Brian Gilbertson, the long-lost uncle of Milly's who she had recently met, was out looking for the missing girl and was in the car park of Collingwood Place when a man with a dog walked near him. 'Brian Gilbertson described the man with the dog as reasonably thick-set, stocky build, about 5 foot 11 inches to 6 foot in height, shortish, dark-coloured hair, which he thought was between one and two inches in length. The man was white and aged between 30 and 40 and he walked with an air of confidence. This we suggest is not a bad description of the defendant's general features. The prosecution say that you can conclude from all this that the man Gilbertson saw in the early hours was the defendant who had returned to Collingwood Place with the dog. The question for you is why, on that night of all nights, he should decide to get up in the early hours to go back to the flat in Collingwood Place in order to sleep in. We suggest that was an excuse he made to Emma in order to legitimise a return to the flat … So why return to Collingwood Place in the dead of night? To walk the dog? To lie in? If the prosecution is right that he abducted and killed Milly Dowler, then he had to dispose of her body and clean up.'

Mr Altman said Bellfield knew a man called Malcolm Ward. At Bellfield's request, Ward helped him clear out belongings from Collingwood Place on the day after Milly disappeared. Emma Mills returned to Collingwood Place after the house-sitting was over. 'Bellfield dropped her off at the flat in her car but did not go inside with her. When she entered the bedroom she saw that the sheets were off the bed. There was no duvet cover, sheet or pillowcases. Only the duvet was left in the middle of the bed. Because of this she rang the defendant on his mobile phone and she asked him about what she had seen. His response was to say that the dog had had an accident and he had "chucked it all". Emma did not believe him because the dog did not have accidents. He told her he had put the soiled linen in the rubbish. She checked some of the bins where there was rubbish but found nothing there. But she did not check them all.

'Emma Mills and Bellfield moved out of 24 Collingwood Place during the weekend of Saturday, 23 March,' said Mr Altman. 'As I have made plain, Emma had not intended moving back to Little Benty for another month. Indeed, on 1 March 2002, she telephoned Jackson's letting agents purporting to terminate the lease which, if it had been accepted, would have meant them leaving the flat at the end of April or beginning of May – which was entirely consistent with her intentions. But Carmen Lippold, the letting agent, told her that the notice had to be in writing. So Emma obliged by writing a letter giving two months' notice to quit with effect from 1 March 2002. However, because the notice to quit had to be calculated from a rent day, in this case the 21st of the month, the agent calculated it to begin from 21 March – which meant the earliest date she was contractually able to quit the flat was in fact 20 May 2002. Two months after the defendant told her they were to move. You may wish to ask the question, why was the defendant in such a rush at this time of all times to make an unplanned and accelerated move away from Collingwood Place? In fact, this was identical to how he was to behave following the murders of Marsha McDonnell and Amelie Delagrange in

2003–2004 when he left home with his family to take sudden holidays or move them from home, as we shall see.

'What then became of the red Daewoo Nexia? According to Emma Mills, they used the red Daewoo Nexia to transport most of their belongings from Collingwood Place to Little Benty. On 29 March 2002, the red Daewoo Nexia was reported as having been stolen and it has never been traced. According to Emma, the defendant had told her that he had been at his uncle Charlie Brazil's sister's house in Hounslow and he had left the Daewoo Nexia outside their house in the road whilst he was out for a drink. He told her he had returned the following day to pick it up but the car had disappeared. He did not appear particularly bothered about its theft. He claimed that inside the car at the time of its theft were a coat and some boots recently purchased by him.'

Mr Altman explained to the jury the significance of the 'stolen' car when he said, 'Because whoever it was abducted and then killed Milly had to have transported her body the 25 miles or so into Hampshire to dispose of her remains – and for that a vehicle was needed. If the defendant abducted and killed her, then he needed the red Daewoo Nexia to dispose of the body, and so the disappearance of that car so soon thereafter is no coincidence – and you can conclude that it was no theft that caused a cheap car to vanish without trace. Like the Ford Courier van that was probably to connect Bellfield to the murder of Amelie Delagrange two years later and which suffered an identical fate to the Nexia, the defendant feared with justification that the red Daewoo Nexia linked him inexorably to Milly's abduction and murder. And so he got rid of it – so completely and so permanently that a huge police inquiry to find it has met a dead end.'

After recounting the details of the discovery of Milly's body in the woods six months later, Mr Altman then explained how Bellfield came to have knowledge of Yateley Heath Woods. 'Johanna Collings was in a relationship with the defendant for about four years from 1994 to 1998. She knew of Emma Mills before beginning her relationship with him who, as we know, began her relationship with him in 1995–1996. Johanna Collings, like Emma, had met the defendant in Rocky's nightclub in Cobham where he had been a doorman. When they were together they lived at her home in Strawberry Hill, Twickenham. He fathered her two children born in February 1996 and the other July 1997. By the time her second child had been born, however, she and the defendant had broken up. When he was with Johanna Collings, he would make many trips to Blackbushe market and Blackbushe car auctions, just north of Yateley. He would also attend horse trials at Yateley with Johanna Collings, who was a keen show jumper. He would follow her horse van in his car. On a site visit to the area with police in 2006, Johanna Collings pointed out a layby on the A30 before the Gibraltar barracks which they would pull into and where they would walk her dogs. That area is known as Yateley common. On another site visit she pointed out to the police Minley Warren and Minley

Road where they would park and then go into the woods, in the very area where Milly's body was discovered.

'On 6 July 2005, the defendant was arrested on suspicion of the murder and kidnapping of Milly Dowler. He was interviewed under caution that day and the next in the presence of his solicitor but he answered "No comment" to the questions asked of him. However, in one instance, he asked the interviewing officers if they were alleging that he had returned to Collingwood Place in the early hours. When he was told they were, you may think hedging his bets, he proffered the view that there was sufficient CCTV on the Birds Eye building – and the roads would be empty – to see a vehicle pulling into Collingwood Place at that time of night. He suggested also the police would have 24 hours' recordings. In fact, as I have told you, the Birds Eye system did not record over 24 hours so there is no CCTV footage which can say that his car did or did not pass by the cameras that night – and other CCTV opportunities were lost due to the passage of time.'

Mr Altman also told the jury the details of Bellfield's 2008 convictions (the Criminal Justice Act of 2003 having made it possible for bad character evidence to be placed before a jury) and he first addressed the murder of Marsha McDonnell. Having described the circumstances of her attack in Kingston, he continued by referring to the Vauxhall Corsa seen near the bus Marsha had alighted from. Bellfield's Corsa was 'one of a very small number of Vauxhall Corsas which could not be eliminated as having been captured by the CCTV system on the bus.

Following the incident, the defendant sold the Vauxhall Corsa cheaply, even though there was substantial credit outstanding in relation to the finance of it, and, equally suddenly, he took his family on holiday abroad to Tenerife. The permission of the older child's school was needed because, rather than go away over the half-term holiday, the defendant insisted they go away during term time, from 14 February to 21 February 2003, which was the week before the half-term holiday. Despite the defendant's view that the school did not need to be informed about the holiday, Emma Mills notified the school on or about Monday, 10 February that there was to be a family holiday between 14 February and 21 February 2003. That holiday took place some ten days after Marsha's murder.'

Moving on to the attempted murder of Kate Sheedy, Altman said, 'The vehicle which ran Kate over was a white Toyota Previa people carrier with blacked-out windows – exactly the type of vehicle that the defendant had possession of at this time, bearing the registration K855 EFL. That vehicle was recovered by police in November 2004 from 10 Craneswater, Hayes, which was the home address of James McCarthy, now deceased, and his family. McCarthy had bought the car in July 2004. Bellfield had purchased the Previa in May 2003 and sold it to an acquaintance in Christmas 2003 but he had an arrangement to use it and was still using it at the time of the attempted murder of Kate Sheedy. Bellfield took the Previa to a car valeting service in June 2004 to be cleaned a month before it was sold on to McCarthy by the person he had the car-sharing arrangement with … As I have already said, at the time the defendant was stalking and attacking Kate, the mobile phone the defendant was then using was silent. It made and received no calls, leading to an inference that it was off.'

The night that Amelie Delagrange met her death on Twickenham Green was also relived by Mr Altman. He said that a bus camera had spotted her at 10.01pm. 'She was still walking on the east side of Hampton Road and approaching a pedestrian crossing which runs across Hampton Road by Twickenham Green – past the cricket pavilion on the Green. She had to cross Hampton Road to get home. The CCTV imagery also revealed the presence of a white Ford Courier van cruising the area from about 9.30 that evening until its speedy departure from the Twickenham Green area, south, at about 10.08pm. The CCTV footage shows that at some point between 10.00pm and about 10.05pm the van came to park by the Green – close to the pavilion – but it had departed by 10.08pm.

'It was during that period, as Amelie was crossing the Green, that she was attacked and struck over the head by a blunt instrument. She died from her injuries. As had been the case with Marsha McDonnell, Amelie's death resulted from the effects of the severe injury to her head. There was no evidence of any defence injury. The location of the blow was suggestive of her having been struck from behind. It appears that the driver of the van, in other words the defendant, had spotted Amelie in Hampton Road, waited for her in his van by the Green and when she walked across the Green he had intercepted and attacked her, stealing her possessions, before returning to the van and driving off. After leaving Twickenham Green, CCTV from a variety of sources showed the van travelling at speed towards Walton, where some or all of Amelie's personal effects were disposed of in the Thames at Walton, under Walton bridge. These included her mobile phone, which last registered to a cell in Walton at 10.22pm. The same van was then captured by CCTV travelling north some 26 minutes later in a direction that would lead to West Drayton, where evidence showed Bellfield in fact did go.

'Technical examination showed the vehicle in the relevant imagery to be a Ford Courier with the index P610 XCN, which Bellfield owned at this time. Other evidence, including other CCTV, linked Bellfield to the use of that van in August 2004. Call data for the telephone that the defendant was using on Thursday, 19 August 2004 was examined and it was found that for the period of – and following – the incident his telephone had been silent, as I have told you, suggesting – we allege – he had switched it off, repeating the pattern we saw over those two days in March 2002 and in May 2004.

'Cell-siting of the telephone on the morning of Friday, 20 August showed that the phone moved to the Iver area, but then, from about 9.37am, the phone and with it, its user – Bellfield – moved west towards the Slough area and then, as I have already told you, north through Buckinghamshire and then Hertfordshire, reaching the Potters Bar/Enfield area by about 11.30am – travelling around at least part of the M25, just as he had on 25 March 2002. Also, following the murder, not unlike the Tenerife holiday in February 2003, the defendant made an unexpected arrangement for his family to stay with friends out of the area in Kent, where they lived for a few days. There was evidence that the defendant had the suspect white Ford Courier van with him but, as I have said, it – just like the red Daewoo Nexia before it – was to disappear, never to be traced.'

Mr Altman then dealt, crucially, with what he termed the 'features of similarity' in the cases involving Bellfield. 'We say that when you analyse the defendant's offending and compare it with what we know about the allegations you are being asked to try – while no two cases are committed identically – there are similarities surrounding the offences and in the defendant's behaviour thereafter which provide evidence in each case that he, to the exclusion of anyone else in the world, was the offender.' Altman began by looking at geographical links. 'The offences of which the defendant was convicted in 2008 all took place within the west London area and he had close links to them all – but the overview map showing Shepperton and Walton, where the offences you are trying occurred, show that they were close by. All of these offences took place within the west and south-west part of the M25 in locations surrounding the M3 and A316 corridor into and out of London.

'The scene of Marsha McDonnell's murder in February 2003

is Priory Road, Hampton, to the south of Twickenham, where the defendant fled south in the white Ford Courier van after killing Amelia Delagrange. The defendant had links with Hampton. His mother lived not very far away in South Road, Hanworth, his sister Lindy kept horses in stables nearby. An aunt, now deceased, also lived in the Hampton area. Bellfield was between 1998 and 2002 a registered company director at an accommodation address in Mount Mews in Hampton. He also had links to the Twickenham area. As you may remember me telling you, he had lived there in the past with both Johanna Collings and Emma Mills.

'The attack on Kate Sheedy in May 2004 was in Worton Road, Isleworth, which sits north of Twickenham. Kate had taken an H22 bus from Twickenham whose route was along the A305 Hampton Road through Whitton to Worton Road where she was run over. The defendant had connections, through the acquisition of car finance in 2002, with Worton Road, as I have told you. That is where he bought on finance the Vauxhall Corsa from which he targeted Marsha McDonnell getting off a bus in February 2003.

'These were areas familiar to Bellfield. Local knowledge, you may think, is a sensible qualification for an attacker and attacks of this kind, where a quick – hopefully trouble-free – escape is needed. The scene of the approach to Rachel Cowles is three miles away from Walton. The defendant had worked in Shepperton and was familiar with it. It was on the route to his mother's house in Hanworth and West Drayton further north.

According to Susan Shaw, who knew the defendant, in about 2002 the defendant worked as a driver for a couple of weeks for New Lion Cars cab company in Shepperton. Emma Mills recalls Bellfield working for a cab firm in Shepperton. Shepperton was, of course, the location for the attempt to get Rachel Cowles into a red car. The defendant had clear links with Walton – not least Collingwood Place and Station Avenue, the scene of Milly Dowler's abduction. It was in the Thames at Walton he was two years later to dispose of Amelie Delagrange's personal effects. We do not, of course, overlook the fact that, in the case of Milly Dowler, the defendant was not in an area in which he had no business, as such, to be. However, you will also recall that at the time he – together with Emma and the two children – were house-sitting for Christine Hawgood over 13 miles north of Walton, in West Drayton. And so there was no obvious reason for him to be in Walton over those days.'

The next element of similarity was the focus on what were called young female stranger victims. 'All of the defendant's victims were vulnerable young women or lone girls. He deliberately targeted each of them in his vehicle, stalking well-lit buses at night, which was but one secure way in which he was able to see and identify female victims, buses from which these girls alighted alone on the street to get home – Marsha and Kate – or in the case of Amelie she having alighted from the wrong bus stop as he cruised the streets chancing upon her walking home alone. Or by chancing upon lone schoolgirls walking home alone on the street in broad daylight: Rachel and Milly in 2002 – the first of the two 2002 cases involving him spotting Rachel from a car. Rachel Cowles was a little short of her 12th birthday, Milly Dowler was 13 years old, Marsha McDonnell was 19 years old, Kate Sheedy 18 years old and Amelie Delagrange 22 years old. Rachel and Milly were schoolgirls who were walking home alone. Marsha, Kate and Amelie were returning home alone from a night out. Each of his 2003–2004 victims was a stranger to him. In the case of Rachel Cowles, it is obvious from what the man said that he was a stranger to her and was trying to trick her into believing he was a new neighbour to gain her trust. You are entitled to conclude that Milly was abducted by a stranger, there being no evidence to the contrary.'

Mr Altman discussed the use of vehicles. 'It was a common feature of the offences of which the defendant was convicted that he used vehicles – to target Marsha, Kate and Amelie and then flee the scene. The defendant used a vehicle associated with him in his approach, we suggest, to Rachel. Of course, in all those instances he was not at or close to home. So the vehicle had a dual function for him: first, it operated as a safe haven from which he was able to target his victims and, secondly, it was a perfect means of escape. In each of the cases for which he was convicted in 2008, he disposed or effectively divested himself of the vehicle that connected him to the offence. In the case of Milly, there is no evidence of any vehicle connection to the approach to and abduction of Milly by anyone. But if the prosecution is right about it, the defendant did not need any vehicle to target Milly or to flee the scene immediately because he had the safe haven of his flat only yards away. But, of course, he did use the red Daewoo to flee – and we see that on the Birds Eye CCTV system … and the red Daewoo car was reported stolen and, as you know, it has never been recovered, despite a massive police hunt for it.

'You are entitled also to consider the speed with which the defendant operated to kill Marsha and Amelie and attempted to do so in Kate's case and the brazen way in which he approached Rachel – if the prosecution is right about it. The speed and nature of approach can explain how Milly disappeared so suddenly and without it being witnessed or at least recognised for what it was. The relative quiet of Station Avenue at the time handed an advantage to the attacker. Speed of action and decisiveness, you may think, had to be important in the abduction of Milly Dowler. In this instance, there is evidence – from the combination of the evidence of Katherine Laynes and the CCTV material, if you accept it – that Milly disappeared from the street very suddenly and without any opportunity to scream or call for help. In that respect, the speed of her abduction resonates with the speed and decisiveness with which the defendant later attacked his other unwitting victims.

'The attacks on Marsha, Kate and Amelie were all characterised by a sudden use of violence which, at its end, was of very great ferocity. There being no actual or attempted sexual interference with any of the victims, the defendant's motivation for killing or attempting to kill was not obvious – but it is, you may conclude, at the very least consistent with someone who harbours very great animosity towards women of the description of those victims and who goes on to act upon it.'

Next Mr Altman dealt with Bellfield's behaviour at the time of the offences.

'It so happens that, on consecutive days, the defendant had turned off his mobile telephone for the period in which the Rachel Cowles and Milly Dowler offences were being committed. His phone was silent, consistent – we suggest – with it being off when he attacked Kate Sheedy in May 2004 and then Amelie Delagrange in August 2004. This is no coincidence. As I have already commented, radio silence allowed him to operate untroubled by inbound calls, in particular from Emma, but more importantly it avoided the authorities – or so he thought – locating him through his mobile phone at the point in time he was committing the offences, thus indicating a high degree of forensic awareness. The evidence is that, following Milly's abduction and murder, the defendant accelerated the departure of him and his family from Collingwood Place. You can conclude that he was reacting to what he knew had taken place at that location and he was putting distance between the place where Milly had disappeared and himself. In a similar way, as I have said, he suddenly took his family on holiday to Tenerife following the murder of Marsha McDonnell and he moved his family down to Kent following the murder of Amelie Delagrange.

'So those are features of similarity which, we say, point to these offences being the work of one man, that man being this defendant, Levi Bellfield. First, the fact his 2008 convictions postdate what he is accused of here matters not because, if the prosecution is right about his involvement in the offences you are trying, all of these offences took place within a period of two years. Moreover, those convictions provide an unchallengeable historical record against which you can judge the evidence of the indicted offences. Without it you could not understand the full implications of the evidence overall: how it might be that in broad daylight and within a flash, a 13-year-old girl can be plucked from the street – unless you knew that the defendant was capable of and had indeed gone on to kill, not once but twice and nearly a third time, with decisive speed and without real concern for being seen to do so.

'Secondly, the evidence allows you to conclude that it would be contrary to common sense to say that there must have been two men with such capabilities appearing by happenstance in the same place at the same time. Thus, you may wish to consider how likely it is that there were two such men capable of committing murder, disposed to behave in exactly the same way, in the same place, at the very same time. Indeed, that two men capable of abduction appeared on consecutive days at around the same time of day on both Wednesday, 20 March and Thursday, 21 March 2002 within three or so miles of each other, you may think no coincidence at all, but point conclusively to the appearance of the same man. In other words, out of a limited number of people with the capacity and opportunity to have committed such offences, Levi Bellfield alone was there, clearly present and highly likely to have done so. So you can ask yourselves whether or not the evidence tending to identify the defendant as the attacker or would-be attacker of each of these girls is a matter explicable purely by coincidence.

'It is, we say, not contrary to common sense that a man so implicated by the evidence of the indicted counts should also go on to commit murderous attacks on young women who were complete strangers to him, as this man did, within a matter of just over two years. Putting it another way, the fact that the defendant has shown himself to be a killer of two women and – but for her good fortune – there would have been a third, within a little over two years from the attempted abduction of Rachel Cowles and the abduction and murder of Milly Dowler in March 2002, provides you with conclusive evidence that the defendant has the capacity to behave suddenly and murderously towards young women for no obvious reason. It means also that you can exclude the suggestion that these are mere unfortunate coincidences, and that Levi Bellfield is simply the unfortunate victim of circumstance.'

Nearing the end of the opening speech he spread over two days, Mr Altman said, 'You can decide that there are similarities in how this man behaves during and after committing grave offences that will help you conclude that we are looking at the work of one and the same man and that that man is Levi Bellfield. The fact that the prosecution cannot identify his motive, other than what we suggest is an obvious animosity to young women and, in this case towards girls of school age, is in truth of no importance. The prosecution have no burden of proving an offender's motive. There may be none or there may be many different and irrational motives but proof of them by the prosecution is no requirement.

'There is no evidence how Milly was abducted, or kidnapped – which only proves the skill and artifice of the offender. However, it matters not because you can be quite sure she was abducted and indeed murdered. That the offender succeeded in concealing the mechanism of abduction and death does not mean he cannot be tried and convicted of them. Otherwise, the more successful the offender was at concealing his deeds, then the more chance he would have of escaping his responsibility. Lack of proof of the mechanism of abduction and of the cause of death in Milly's case is therefore no impediment to prosecution and conviction for them. No sensible system of criminal justice works that way and this one certainly does not.

'The fact is there is no evidence to assist you as to how Milly was abducted. If you are satisfied the defendant tried to abduct Rachel the very day before Milly disappeared, as we say on the whole of the evidence you can be, then in her case he used a trick. Whilst the prosecution have to prove that the defendant abducted and murdered Milly, it has no obligation to prove precisely how she was abducted or where she was killed or even the precise mechanism of death – in other words, how she died. You may think, the more resourceful the offender, the less likely it is he will be caught if he can avoid it – and one means of not being caught is by acting swiftly and leaving little or no trace.

'If, as the prosecution say, the evidence shows that Milly did disappear from the part of Station Avenue where Katherine Laynes last saw her, then her abductor had to be both resourceful and a little fortunate in that no one saw it – or no one saw it for what it really was. So the kidnapping of Milly Dowler was, you may think, executed with an air of confidence by someone with the skill or artifice – and perhaps even the muscle – to pull it off without being noticed. After all, if you are satisfied on the evidence that Milly could not have got into a car without it being obvious – and such an event was simply not captured on the Birds Eye CCTV system – and that she never walked past the Birds Eye building cameras on either side of the road, then someone managed to abduct her from that part of Station Avenue. If not by force then by deception or some such ruse. If that is right, the unassailable fact is that that someone managed successfully to achieve it without being seen. The only question is who? We say you can be quite satisfied that the [would-be] abductor of Rachel Cowles and the abductor and killer of Milly Dowler was this defendant, Levi Bellfield and no one else. Whether that proposition is right will be for you to say having heard the evidence.'

It had been a dramatic speech of almost epic proportions from Mr Altman. Remarkably, the evidence and events of the ensuing weeks in court number eight managed to overshadow it.

CHAPTER 10

Levi Bellfield was dressed casually for his 'day out'. He had on a pair of Nike trainers, pale-blue jeans and a grey jumper with yellow sleeves. On Thursday, 13 May, the judge, jury and lawyers visited the places where Mr Altman said Bellfield committed his crimes. They looked at Walton station and the cafe where Milly ate chips and then took the route that she took that afternoon nine years earlier. When they reached the bus stop from which Milly had last been spotted, Bellfield stood under some nearby trees and, relaxed in his manner, spoke with his defence team. Then they all moved the 32 yards to the door to the block housing 24 Collingwood Place, where the jury had been told that Milly no doubt met her death. They continued down the road, past the Birds Eye factory towards the traffic lights at the intersection en route to her home.

Earlier, they had been to the scene three miles away in Upper Halliford Road, Shepperton, where Rachel Cowles had been approached by the man in a red car. It was Rachel who was to be the first witness in the trial when it resumed at the Old Bailey the next day. The former Bishop Wand Church of England School pupil was by now a smartly dressed, bespectacled young woman. She told of the day she was approached as she walked home from school. 'I was alone. A car pulled up and its window was wound down on the passenger side. The car was red, non-metallic. I just glanced through the back window and remember seeing magazines strewn across the floor behind the passenger seat.' Rachel said she believed the car may have been driven up the opposite side of the dual carriageway before doubling back towards her. The engine was running and the driver leaned over to speak to her. 'I saw him from the side and then he turned his face round to me. He was white. My impression was that he was in his thirties to forties. He was skinheaded or bald. His head was rather chubby. He had a gold hoop earring in his left ear … He said to me, "Hello, I have just moved in next door to you. Would you like a lift home?" I said, "No, thank you, I'm all right."'

Later that day, when her mother telephoned the police, young Rachel broke down in tears when she tried to describe what had happened. Rachel's mother Diana told the court, 'As soon as they started asking her questions, she burst into tears. The enormity of it obviously hit home.' It was not until three years later that detectives took a statement and only after Diana had written to the chief constable of Surrey police. She had seen an appeal in 2005 on ITV's breakfast show *GMTV* for a red car. Rachel gave a description of a similar vehicle, including its interior.

On the afternoon of Monday, 16 May, Bob Dowler entered the witness box. His evidence was to be short but dramatic and was soon to be the centre of a nationwide debate over the treatment of witnesses. He began by telling Mr Altman of the events of 21 March and how he had told his family he would be home early that day. 'I said, "Goodbye," and gave them a kiss, particularly Amanda. It was important that I gave her a kiss goodbye. It was a bit of a family habit that I gave her a kiss in the morning. The previous day I had left early and she reminded me that I had not kissed her goodbye the previous morning.'

He confirmed that he had got home about 3.00pm to 3.15pm and that Milly made her call about 4.15pm. He went into his study to work with the door closed, so it was only when his wife and their older daughter Gemma returned that he realised that Milly had not arrived. His wife came into the room while he was on the phone. She put a note on the desk to say she was going out, adding, 'Where's Milly?' After making calls and driving around the area, he called the police.

The cross-examination of Mr Dowler by Bellfield's counsel, Jeffrey Samuels QC, was to cause a storm. Mr Dowler said that a search of the family's home uncovered porn magazines and videos in various rooms and a box of bondage equipment in the attic. Among the items recovered were a rubber hood, a strap and ball gag, and magazines. He also confirmed that his wife Sally had no knowledge of these items. Mr Dowler agreed with the defence barrister he was the focus of police attention in the early days of the investigation but that he initially omitted to tell police his exact movements that day. He later confirmed to the jury he had become aroused by flicking through porn magazines at a motorway service station before going home. The subsequent discovery of bondage equipment led police to suspect him.

Mr Samuels said, 'They were suggesting you may have had something to do with your own daughter's disappearance, weren't they?'

'I believe that may have been the case,' he replied. He told the court he later went back to police and confessed he had misled them. He said Milly had discovered a porn magazine in the bedroom some time earlier but that he didn't think his daughter had found his bondage gear. He told police, 'If she had come across those materials I have no doubt that she would have been very distressed.' It was irresponsible of him, he said, and 'a complete betrayal of her as a father'.

He was questioned three times by police between 26 March and 18 April. They asked him, 'Are you in any way responsible for Milly's disappearance?'

In a response read to the court, he told them, 'The only way I can be responsible is if she had seen some of this material and decided to run away. But I have no other involvement with Milly's disappearance whatsoever. I recognise that leaving material round the property would have caused her distress and may have caused her to run away.' Those comments were made, he said, when it was thought that Milly was just missing. There had been no problems between the two of them after Milly's initial discovery of the porn magazine. The disclosure of the nature of the items found in the Dowlers' bedroom and loft was made to a hushed court. Mr Dowler also told the jury that on returning home during the afternoon of 21 March he had committed a sex act.

At one stage, Mr Dowler was unable to hold back his tears when notes and letters written by Milly and found in her room were read to the court. It was not surprising. He was not the only person in court number eight who struggled to contain their emotions. One note read, 'Dear Daddy and my beautiful mummy, by the time you find this letter I will be gone, up there or down below you. I have always been that way, below other people. I am sorry, you deserve a better daughter so I have left. If anything, you should be happy now, you can concentrate on lovely Gemsy without me getting in the way. You should have had an abortion or at least had me adopted, then at least I would not have made your life hell as well. I think it would be best if you try and forget me. It's nothing you have done. I just feel I had to go. Please don't let any harm get to any of you. Mum and Dad, please look after Gemma. I am sorry but goodbye. Lots of love, as always, your little disappointment, Amanda.'

Police also found a page from another document in Milly's room in which she wrote, 'Jess is a true friend. She is the best. Jess helped me the most with this whole Dad thing.' Her father accepted it was almost certainly a reference to his daughter finding one of his porn magazines.

There was also a poem read by Mr Samuels which Mr Dowler described as 'very sad'. It read, 'I don't know what it is I do, they all just seem to hate me. All they do is slag me off and force everyone against me. I know I am pathetic and helpless and I know I'm not pretty or fit. But what do they have that I haven't? Let's face it, I am just totally s★★★. I know what people think, I know how they feel. Why the f★★★, I don't know. What do I do to make them hate me? Maybe I should just go. Sometimes I think how life would be without me, for Mum and Dad to have a beautiful little girl who is something like Gemma. She would be everything I am not, everything I dream to be, pretty, smart, intelligent, wanted, loved. Then I hit myself and wake up to reality and how bad school's going to be in the morning. I hate it but not nearly as much as I hate myself.'

Bob Dowler, a tall man who walked in an almost military manner, had entered the witness box at 2.00pm and left it at 3.20pm. He had only given evidence for 80 minutes but it had seemed like an eternity as the most intimate details of his life were laid bare. His wife was next to give evidence and this was, if anything, even more harrowing. Sally Dowler looked tense and nervous as she entered the witness box but at first seemed to be in control of her emotions as she told how, in November 2001, the family had discovered a 'lost' relative. This was an uncle for

Milly, publican Brian Gilbertson. Milly's grandmother had given birth to him at 16 and they had just been reunited. The weekend before Milly vanished, the family had gone to a fun run in Essex where the uncle lived. 'It was really lovely,' said Sally. 'At the pub afterwards Brian had organised a party and there was a saxophonist and a keyboard player and they asked Milly to play with them. She really, really enjoyed it.' Her daughter said it had been 'one of the best days of her life'.

Later in the week, Milly had been with friends to see the Pop Idol concert with Gareth Gates and Will Young, and she had ironed her jeans – her first attempt at ironing. It caused hilarity in the family. Mrs Dowler also talked about the tutorial she had to give after school finished on 21 March and how she was going to take her daughters home. 'Milly came to see me to say that she had done her work at lunchtime and she did not fancy waiting round for an hour. She was going to get the train from Weybridge station, which was fine.' Mrs Dowler got home about 4.40–4.45pm, had a cup of tea and got washed and changed for the babysitting stint. 'I remember the hall was remarkably tidy,' she told the court. Normally it would have had Milly's bags and shoes in it.

Sally Dowler also discussed her daughter's discovery in the Dowlers' bedroom. She said to her mother, 'Mum, I have something to tell you.' Milly had gone to get something out of the chest and the whole drawer had come out, revealing the pornography. Mrs Dowler had not known what was there but she told her daughter, 'It does not mean Daddy does not love Mummy.' She said Milly's attitude to her husband did not change afterwards and nor did the girl ever mention finding anything else of a similar nature. 'I was shocked to find them there as well. She was upset. I shouted at him and we had an argument and he said he would remove them.'

At one stage, when Mr Samuels was referring to the 'extreme' nature of the pornography, Mr Altman rose to his feet to ask how necessary that line of enquiry was.

Sally Dowler was reminded that she told police that she had noticed 'a slight change' in her daughter for a while before things went back to normal. She told the court she was not sure when the incident had taken place. It could have been a few months before the abduction or even the previous summer. 'It was ten years ago. It was really hard to recall it. Over the space of ten years, I had a nervous breakdown and it is very difficult for me to recall it. If she had any problems, she would have come and talked to me about them. I think we had a good relationship.' Mr Dowler told his wife about the bondage gear in the loft before police searched it and that was the first that Mrs Dowler knew of what was up there, she said. Crying, she explained that Milly would not have discovered the other items. 'I can't recall Milly ever going in the loft. She did not like the dark and it was all dusty with spiders.'

Questioned about the poems and the 'Goodbye' letter, she said she had not seen them before. As a teacher, she thought they were not unusual because girls of that age often wrote similar things in their diaries. Mr Samuels asked her about Milly's email address, sexmeslow@hotmail.com. Mrs Dowler said Milly had told her that all her friends had addresses like that. Asked if she had any reason to believe Milly was suicidal or was thinking of running away, Mrs Dowler insisted in a loud, practically breaking voice, 'No, we were a happy family.' When Mr Samuels asked if the letters suggested that the Dowlers favoured Gemma, then 16, and paid her more attention, Mrs Dowler broke down. Eventually, she regained her composure and replied, 'I was not aware of that. I was shown the note and it was not true. She never said that to me.' Mrs Dowler said that the note from Milly painted a picture of her daughter which she did not recognise. 'I would not describe her as a dark and depressing person.'

After Milly disappeared, Mrs Dowler tried to remember everything that had happened, she said. Sometime later, after being up all night, she had telephoned her police liaison officer to beg for the third time to be hypnotised in case she had left anything out. She thought she had driven past Milly standing with a group of boys near Station Avenue but was not sure if it was on the fateful day. 'I was thinking over and over again, trying to remember the minutest detail,' she said. 'I was driving myself mad. I can remember saying I need to be hypnotised in order to recall something. I didn't know if it was that afternoon. I had got so confused. I was so desperate.'

When she was questioned again by Mr Altman, she spoke of the family holiday they all had in Mexico and Cuba. 'It was an awesome holiday and I am so glad we did it,' she said and insisted, 'She was happy. We were a happy family.' She said the last sentence as though she wanted not just the courtroom but the entire world to know. Throughout this witness-box ordeal, Bellfield looked on unconcerned. The Old Bailey matron had to be called at one stage to ensure Mrs Dowler was medically fit to continue. Yet Bellfield showed no emotion as she finished giving evidence, collapsed into the arms of the female usher and had to be helped out of court by her husband and a police liaison officer. No one watching, apart from Bellfield, could have failed to be moved by her appearance.

At least Gemma Dowler was spared the ordeal of giving evidence from the witness box. She sat in court holding her father's arm as her statement was read by Mr Altman. She had walked into the family home that afternoon after school and said she called out, '"Amanda, Amanda, where are you?" and I got no response.' She phoned some of Milly's friends and her father went out to look for the youngster. 'I said to him, "I think this is getting serious now. I think we should call the police." I knew immediately that something bad had happened to Milly, that she had been abducted. There was no way that she would have gone off. I knew Milly wouldn't go out without telling Mum or Dad. I rang Milly's mobile. It was switched off so I left a message.'

A series of Milly's friends – schoolgirls at the time but now young women – gave evidence either from the witness box or in the form of statements. Danielle Sykes told the jury she persuaded

Milly to get off their train a stop early to have chips. Blonde Danielle, now 23, said Milly was in a good mood as they walked from their school to Weybridge station and caught the 3.26pm train. She recalled, 'I started to say goodbye. I hugged her goodbye and went to go our separate ways. But I said something along the lines of, "Would you like to come and get chips with me at the cafe?" It was something I had done previously. She said, "No, I had better not." I jokingly said, "Oh, fine, then." She changed her mind. She said, "Oh, no. Actually, I will come. I have nothing better to do." Milly had only once before decided to get off the train to eat at the Travellers Cafe and then walk home, she said.

The girls bought a 90p portion of chips each and then discussed boys they liked at school, a gig they had planned to go to the following day and boys they knew who were playing in the band. 'She was cracking jokes and being her usual self.' Ms Sykes said that Milly was 'one of the funniest people I have ever met. She was always trying to make people laugh. When she was happy she was very happy and infectious … she valued her friendships and her family a lot. I saw her as a confident person but not in a bad way at all. She was sensible. She would know the risk of talking to strangers as well.'

Danielle was joined by her older sister Natalie, who had finished college for the day. Eventually the girls all left the cafe, the sisters going in a different direction from Milly. 'I gave her a hug and asked her would she be all right walking home on her own and she replied, "Why, yes, I will be absolutely fine."' Milly had some time earlier discussed finding the porn belonging to her father, and Ms Sykes said, 'She said that she was disappointed and weirded out but then no one wants to think of their parents in that light.'

The next witness was Hannah McDonald, who told of a half-hearted attempt by Milly to slash her wrists after she was bullied at school. She said Milly was depressed about being called 'big nose' by school bullies. Name-calling by pupils at Heathside 'upset Milly greatly', the court heard. Ms McDonald said, 'Just like any 13-year-old she would take it to heart more than an adult would. Looking back, it was pretty trivial and there was no need for her to get upset by it.'

Mr Samuels asked if Milly had confided in her over her wrist-cutting. She replied, 'With a dinner knife, yes. She told me it wasn't a secret within the family. Milly did like to exaggerate things and she only told me a year or so after the event. She was a joker. That is the best way I could describe her. If you were down, she would try to make you smile. She had a funny voice she used to do. She would always make you laugh. I think sometimes she used humour to mask that she was lacking in self-confidence.'

The court heard from Jessica Lauchlan about Milly's reaction to finding pornography. Ms Lauchlan sat next to Milly in class and said in a statement, 'She said it was really worrying because "I did not think my dad was like that". I got the impression Milly found a few magazines but did not say anything of the contents other than that there was a female on the front. Milly was quite upset about it because she was quiet all day. She was normally loud and nutty.'

Katherine Laynes, now 24, told how she was the last person to see Milly alive. Ms Laynes gave her account of sitting at the bus shelter on the northern side of Station Avenue when she saw Milly on the opposite side of the road. She said, 'We both made eye contact. I didn't wave or anything but I thought we both recognised each other.' Milly walked out of her view, obscured by a poster on the bus shelter and Ms Laynes boarded her bus. She said, 'I was looking out for Milly, expecting to see her, but I didn't.' As the bus stopped at traffic lights, she looked again. 'I remember it was quite weird I had not seen her. I had a look but I still didn't see her,' she said.

Milly's friends were not, of course, the only ones to give evidence in Bellfield's trial. Brian Gilbertson, her newly discovered uncle from Ongar in Essex, had earlier that day received the freedom of the City of London and had been due to have dinner with Milly's grandmother. But when the family heard she was missing he drove to Surrey and decided to walk the mile-long route she would have taken home from the station. He took with him a torch and a baseball bat. And in the early hours of 22 March he came across a man with a dog near Collingwood Place. That man, said the prosecution, was Levi Bellfield returning to the scene of the crime to dispose of any remaining evidence.

Mr Gilbertson said, 'I saw a person walking towards me, a male.

He was approximately 5 foot 11 inches to 6 foot 1 inch.' The man was 'stocky and well built. I believe his age was between 30 and 40 years old. His hair style was shortish hair. I would estimate it to be no more than about two inches long. The clothing this person was wearing was very dark and unrecognisable. He was approaching me in a concerning fashion. I felt it was an intimidating manner. He was walking towards me very confidently with the air of someone who was going to say something or do something to me.' The man was not carrying anything but had a dog very close by. It was not on a lead but trotted just six to eight feet away and was obviously with him. 'He was walking quite quickly towards me and within 10 to 15 feet away from where we were going to pass, he veered off.' Mr Gilbertson said that at the time it appeared to him that he was by an entrance to a block of flats. 'When I revisited it during daylight hours, it was, clearly, an area where there were refuse bins and where they put all the rubbish out.'

As had been the case in his first trial, the women in Bellfield's life were to play key courtroom roles, none more so than Emma Mills, mother of three of his children. They had been together at the time of Milly's disappearance and she told the jury of his behaviour around 21 March and afterwards. Slim, dark-haired Ms Mills gave evidence from behind a screen, as she had in the first trial, to avoid eye contact with Bellfield.

On the day Milly vanished, Ms Mills, Bellfield and their two children were staying at a friend's house, she said. She had been trying to get hold of him all day but his phone was switched off. 'He disappeared. His mobile was off. I was trying to get in touch with him because I didn't have any money and I needed to get some bits from the shop. Normally, he would ring me or I would ring him on and off during the day to see what I was doing. He didn't ring me at all until later on. I didn't see him past lunchtime.' She said it was unusual for her not to be in contact with Bellfield who was then not working during the day. Eventually, she had a 40-second conversation with him at 5.38pm and a longer call later that evening. 'I don't remember the actual conversation but I know how it probably went with me asking where he was all that time and when he was coming back,' she said.

Bellfield returned to the friend's house between 10.00-11.00pm. 'He was wearing different clothes from those he had on in the morning. They would have been from the flat in Walton. I think he got a takeaway and some lagers. He had had a drink but he was not drunk.' Asked if she put any questions to him, Ms Mills answered, 'I did – but I would never get a straight answer. And even if he did tell me something I would never know if it was the truth.' She woke up in the early hours to find him getting dressed. 'It was around three or four in the morning and he said he was going back to the flat to have a lie-in. He took the dog with him. He just walked out of the room. He said something along the lines of, "I will see you later."'

Bellfield called Ms Mills to say he would pick her up with the children to return to Collingwood Place. He soon started urging her to leave the flat in Walton. She said, 'He said that he didn't want to be in the flat any more. We didn't have to wait for the lease to end. He didn't want to wait. I said, "We can't live in there [Little Benty]." He said, "Oh, you don't want to come back," twisting it on me, pushing me into thinking it's a good idea, trying to get me to go back.' Eventually, she gave in to his demands, but when she returned to Collingwood Place to pack she noticed something strange. 'There were no sheets or pillow cases on the bed. No duvet cover. I rang him. He said the dog had had an accident on the bed. I didn't believe him for a second. I said, "Why would she do that? When did it happen?" He said he put the sheets in the rubbish because they could not be washed.' Ms Mills said Bellfield's bull terrier, Shy, would 'never' have soiled the bed. She looked in the bins outside but could see no linen, she said. The next day – the day after Milly disappeared – she returned to Little Benty. She also said that Bellfield told her about the theft of her red Daewoo, shortly after Milly's death and she claimed for it on her insurance policy.

During her long spell in the witness box, Emma Mills told of a bizarre comment Bellfield made to her a week after Milly vanished. They had spoken about her before as the case had received massive media coverage as it was local. This time it came up as she was decorating. 'I was asking him again about the Thursday he'd gone off because I thought he was with another woman. I was just painting. He said, "Oh, why do you keep going on? What, do you think I've done Milly?" I didn't ask him. It's just so awful,' said Ms Mills. 'I was so used to him making horrible remarks and jokes about things. I just thought, It's disgusting, not even funny.'

Mr Altman asked, 'Had you said anything to provoke such a remark?'

She replied, 'No, I was just asking him what he was doing on the Thursday.'

Asked by Mr Samuels why she had had not mentioned Milly Dowler until after Bellfield's arrest in November 2004 and why she did not 'harbour any suspicions', she said, 'I didn't think he'd done it, but when he made that comment it made me think, Why did he make that comment? But I didn't think that he had done it.'

Another woman to deliver her verdict on Bellfield was Emma's mother, Gillian Mills. She was upset when her daughter became pregnant. She said he reminded her of the character Butch Dingle from the soap opera *Emmerdale*. She told the jury, 'I didn't want Emma to have a life with him.' Emma was no longer a 'well-behaved' teenager after she met him, Mrs Mills said. She was besotted with him and became 'belligerent'. 'I had fallen out with her because I didn't like Levi. Emma changed when she was with him. I would describe Levi as a big fat lump with a high-pitched voice for his size.'

Another of Bellfield's ex-lovers, Johanna Collings, took the stand and tellingly described his knowledge of Yateley Heath

Woods. Ms Collings went hunting rabbits with her dogs in the woods and Bellfield attended horse trials in the area with her.

The court heard details of the police operation to catch Milly's killer. DCI Maria Woodall, the officer in charge, was the fifth senior investigating officer since the night of the abduction. Some 54 people – including Bob Dowler – had been investigated before being eliminated. Police had called at 24 Collingwood Place, an address Bellfield also used for credit card fraud, on ten occasions without success and it was only on the 11th visit that they made any contact. By then a new tenant had replaced Bellfield.

On Thursday, 15 June, Mr Samuels rose to his feet and told the court, 'The defence calls no evidence.' Levi Bellfield would not be going in the witness box. There would be no chance for Mr Altman to cross-examine him. That did mean, however, that the prosecutor would begin his closing speech immediately. When Mr Altman did stand up, it was to tell the jury, now reduced to eleven as one of their number had been taken ill during the trial, that the Dowler family life had been laid bare during the preceding five weeks. Gemma Dowler left the courtroom in tears as he spoke. 'No one, absolutely no one in this courtroom other than Mr and Mrs Dowler and Gemma, their surviving daughter, can possibly know or understand what it was like to have lost a child or a sister in the dreadful circumstances they did on that March afternoon, not knowing for month after month what had become of her. But the grieving parents are not on trial here. That fact may have been forgotten. There is only one person on trial in this courtroom. Yet he, unlike the Dowlers, has not had the courage to give you his account.'

The defence suggestion that the Dowlers were in a way a factor in what happened was ridiculous, said Mr Altman. 'This evidence is being used to suggest that Bob Dowler contributed to his daughter's disappearance and her eventual death. There was an implication in cross-examination that Sally Dowler had not dealt with the matter properly so that somehow her inadequate response to it as a mother has also contributed.' Milly's killer was a 'very skilful operator … with the brazenness and resourcefulness' to steal a child without being seen. He must have had quick and ready access to premises nearby. 'That describes one person and one place. That person is Levi Bellfield.'

Reminding jurors that Milly was last seen yards from Bellfield's doorstep, Mr Altman said, 'You can see it would take seconds – seconds – for a big man with a purpose to have manhandled a small girl without screaming into that flat.' Mr Altman said of Bellfield's decision not to give evidence, 'You might reasonably have thought that a man accused of murdering 13-year-old Milly Dowler and of seeking to abduct Rachel Cowles the day before would want to grasp the opportunity of explaining and protesting his innocence, but he has not done so. The reason he has not done so is that he doesn't have an innocent account to give.' He told the jury they must decide their verdicts on 'many strands of circumstantial evidence'.

Mr Samuels said of Bellfield, 'But for his convictions, you may think, he wouldn't be here.' He said the prosecution had 'marshalled and tailored' evidence to fit their 'ludicrous theory'. 'The sad truth is that police are no nearer to solving the mystery of the disappearance of Milly Dowler now in 2011 than they were in 2002 at the time or any time since,' said Mr Samuels. 'The crime that shocked the nation remaining unsolved represents an uncomfortable position. So you may think that prosecuting this defendant, who has little to lose, presents them with an opportunity that gives them everything to gain.'

He asked why Bellfield had not been charged with Milly's murder when he was convicted of the murders of Amelie Delagrange and Marsha McDonnell and the attempted murder of Kate Sheedy. He said the jury might think this reflected the weakness of the case, and that deficiencies of evidence could be covered 'by parading him before you as a convicted murderer, the local serial killer'. The prosecution had tried to make the evidence fit, with the 'pegs whittled away in order that even the square ones can fit into the round holes'. There was undue reliance on Bellfield's convictions and an 'artificial attempt to suggest similarities when in fact none exist'. 'The claims do not stand up to scrutiny. No eyewitnesses, no scientific evidence to link him to her or vice versa. No images on CCTV.'

One courtroom observer pointed out, as the jury retired to consider their verdict, 'It's been a strange trial – the prosecution has no evidence and the defence has no defence.' Not exactly true, of course, but it somehow seemed to sum up the events of that May and June. Nevertheless, there was to be no escape for Bellfield: On the afternoon of Thursday, 23 June the jury unanimously convicted Bellfield of both charges relating to Milly. They could not reach agreement over the abduction of Rachel Cowles and were told to carry on discussing that charge.

Gemma Dowler collapsed in hysterics outside the court when the verdict was announced and, sobbing, she clasped her parents' hands. Court staff rushed to Gemma's aid in the public foyer of the court while her mother was ushered away.

Levi Bellfield's reaction was different. Throughout his trial, his body language sent out messages of contempt for the court. He'd waved and mouthed messages to his family in the public gallery and coughed and shifted in his seat when the various women in his life gave evidence against him. As he walked out of the dock to be taken back to Belmarsh prison for the night, he didn't even look over his shoulder at the court. Very loudly and very ostentatiously he did just one thing: he yawned.

CHAPTER 11

Levi Bellfield didn't even turn up in court the next day. The judge dryly observed to the defence team, 'Your client has indicated that he does not wish to take part in the proceedings.' As in his first trial, Bellfield did not have the courage to appear in front of the judge who was to sentence him.

An avalanche of reports about Bellfield and his violent past – especially in relation to women – had come out the previous night and in that morning's papers. As a result, it was decided that it would be unrealistic for the jury to proceed with its deliberations over Rachel Cowles and they were discharged. But one question lingered on that did not concern Rachel. It was simply this – who had been on trial at the Old Bailey, Levi Bellfield or the Dowlers?

Bob and Sally Dowler had been subjected to an unremitting

series of questions by Jeffrey Samuels QC on Bellfield's behalf. Mr Dowler was asked about the pornography and bondage gear hidden in the house while Sally was asked about favouring one child over the other. There were suggestions that Milly had problems far greater than normal teenage growing pains. The Dowlers were soon to have their say, but the trial judge was first to speak of the questioning they underwent.

Mr Justice Wilkie, sentencing Bellfield in his absence, said that the 2008 convictions marked Bellfield out 'as a cruel and pitiless killer. To this is added the fact that, as on another occasion at this court, he has not had the courage to come into court to face his victims and receive his sentence. He subjected Milly Dowler, a 13-year-old schoolgirl, to what must have been a terrifying ordeal for no reason other than she was at the wrong place at the wrong time and became a target of the unreasoning hatred that was driving him. He robbed her of her promising life. He robbed her family and friends of the joy of seeing her grow up, like her school friends who have given evidence in this court, into a self-confident, articulate and admirable young woman. He treated her in death with total disrespect, depositing her naked body without even a semblance of a burial, in a wood far away from her home, vulnerable to all the forces of nature. Thereby, as he clearly intended, causing her family the appalling anguish for many months of not knowing what had become of her.

'But most cruel of all, in an attempt to divert responsibility from himself, he instructed his lawyers in this trial to expose to the world her most private, adolescent thoughts, secrets and worries and sought to hint that she was a dark, unhappy and troubled person, a proposition which the jury has rejected and which flew in the face of the evidence from her family and many friends. For those of us in court who have been privileged to get to know about her, it is clear that she was a funny, sparky, enthusiastic teenager fully exploring her developing emotional life, just as any intelligent person of her age might. He must have known that. However skilfully and sensitively it was done – and it was – that process could do no other than hugely increase the anguish of her family, particularly her mother Sally Dowler, in ways which were made dramatically clear to all in court. But he has failed in what he intended. Milly's memory will survive and be cherished long after he is forgotten. The only sentence I can pass for the offence of murder is one of life imprisonment and I do.'

Sentencing him to a whole-life term, the judge added, 'I have regard to the aggravating factors identified at that time [of the murder], namely that this was the killing of a child, that he has a substantial record of serious violence and that he engaged in a macabre attempt to conceal her body. I am glad to see that the family of Milly Dowler are in court. My next words are directed to them. No one who has been in court can have been in any doubt that the Dowler family has suffered indescribable agonies, during almost a decade, over the loss of their beloved daughter Milly, for which all our hearts go out to them. In an important sense, this agony may be thought to have culminated in this trial. I appreciate that the trial process has been excruciating for them by the reason of the issues the defendant instructed his lawyers to raise in his defence. I have already commented on that in sentencing him.

'I understand that they feel let down by the trial process in that respect. Unfortunately, given the nature of the defence, it was unavoidable that these issúes be pursued in court. All that I can do is hope that they may in time come to terms with that and that the outcome of the trial may in some small way contribute to their grieving process and assist them in coming to a semblance of closure.'

Outside the Old Bailey, the Dowlers gathered together. They were finally able to express their views over their ordeal. They supported each other, both mentally and physically, as they revealed their feelings in words that merit repeating in full: Sally Dowler said, 'We are relieved to have this verdict returned and would like to thank the jury for their decision. At last the man responsible for the cruel murder of our darling daughter so many years ago has been found guilty. However, for us, the trial has been an awful experience. We have felt that our family, who have already suffered so much, has been on trial as much as Bellfield. We have had to hear Milly's name defamed in court. She has been portrayed as an unhappy, depressed young girl. Ordinary details that any mother would recognise have been magnified into major problems. The Milly we knew was a happy, vivacious, fun-loving girl. Our family life has been scrutinised and laid open for everyone to inspect and comment upon. We have had to lose our right to privacy and sit through day after harrowing day of the trial in order to get a man convicted of a brutal murder.

'To actually see that man in court, a man capable of such a vile and inhuman crime, has been grotesque and distressing for us. The length the system goes to protect his human rights seems so unfair compared to what we as a family have had to endure. I hope whilst he is in prison he is treated with the same brutality he dealt out to his victims and that his life is a living hell. For a mother to bury her child in any circumstances is truly agonising but to bury your child when you know she died in such an appalling way is unutterably awful. The pain and grief, the damage he has done to our family and friends, will never go away. We have just had to learn to live alongside it. A day does not pass when we do not think of her and the life that she might have had.' She thanked police family liaison officers for their 'incredible support', adding, 'After DCI Maria Woodall took charge of the investigation we at last felt that progress was being made and Maria made every attempt to correct some of the mistakes of her predecessors. For this we are very grateful.'

Gemma too was forthright in her views: 'The past few months have been some of the toughest times for the whole family. I can honestly say that the day my mother and father were questioned by the defence QC was the worst day of my life. It is hard to believe but it was worse than when I heard the news that the remains were that of my sister Milly. The way my parents were questioned can only be described as mental torture. Have they not suffered enough? I will remember that day for the rest of my life. Seeing my mum collapse in court and having to be carried out by my father and our family liaison officer. I was waiting to give evidence, so couldn't even comfort my own mother. The way they can portray my lovely sister as a depressed teenager has shocked me terribly – the worst part being that she isn't here to defend herself. To have to listen to that was emotionally scarring. The scales seem to be tipped so much towards the defendant rather than us, the family who have suffered an almighty loss. It feels like we are the criminals and our family has been on trial.'

Gemma redressed the balance by going on to pay her own tribute to Milly. 'She was the best sister anyone could ask for. She was a shoulder for me to cry on, a fashion guru, a person who could make you laugh even when you felt sad and she would light up a room as soon as she entered. She really was a star, and on dark nights I look out at the sky and there almost seems to be a star shining brighter than the rest. I am sure this is Milly watching over me. When this all happened, nine years ago, I was only 16. I had no other choice but to grow up. I feel I missed out on some wonderful teenage years. I waved goodbye to the happy family we were and I realised life would never be the same again. The past nine years have tested our relationship as a family; there have been extremely bad days but we still manage some good days. Sadly, it is those good days when we realise that there is somebody missing and then I will spend the next day feeling guilty for enjoying myself.

'It had taken me a long time to get to some kind of normal life for a 25-year-old but I felt I was getting there. However, now I feel like all my hard work has been undone. I have not been able to go to work for the past couple of weeks as it takes far too much concentration – which I lack as I am under so much stress. I often asked. "Why? Why us, why our family and, most of all, why Milly?" I now know the answer and that is simply Milly was in the wrong place at the wrong time and there is nothing I can do to change that. With regard to the question of justice, in my eyes justice is an eye for an eye. You brutally murder someone then you pay the ultimate price … a life for a life. So in my eyes, no real justice has been done. He took away my beautiful sister and he will now spend the rest of his time living off of taxpayers' money!'

And Bob Dowler, whose lifestyle had been put under microscopic analysis in the witness box, said, 'We are pleased that a guilty verdict has been delivered by the jury and that Levi Bellfield has been convicted of the murder of our daughter. However, we do not see this as true justice for Milly, merely a criminal conviction. My family has had to pay too high a price for this conviction. The pain and agony that we have endured as a family since 21 March 2002 has been compounded by the devastating effects of this trial. Prior to this trial, my family and I had only an ordinary person's understanding of the legal process.

However, during the past seven weeks, our eyes have been well and truly opened. The trial has been a truly mentally scarring experience on an unimaginable scale – you would have to have been there to truly understand. Things that you would not believe could ever happen did in fact happen. During the past nine years, there have been many occasions when the police investigation has left us in despair. The trial has been a truly horrifying ordeal for my family. We have had to relive all the emotions and thoughts of nine years ago when Milly first went missing and was then found murdered. During our questioning, my wife and I both felt as if we were on trial. The questioning of my wife was particularly cruel and inhuman, resulting in her collapse after leaving the stand. We despair of a justice system that is so loaded in favour of the perpetrator of the crime. It has often appeared almost incidental that this is a trial concerning the murder of our daughter.

'We would like to pay tribute to all the witnesses who so courageously gave evidence for the prosecution. This is in stark contrast to the cowardly behaviour of Levi Bellfield who was able to decline to give evidence and chose instead to hide behind his defence QC – to challenge the testimony of every witness. Where is the fairness in a system which allows such behaviour? The defence inferences about myself and my wife were hugely distressing. And yet again Bellfield has been spineless and gutless for not attending his sentencing today. Thank goodness that we have so many close and wider family members and friends who have supported us through the past nine years. Saturday, 25 June would have been Milly's 23rd birthday and as always we will remember the happy, fun-loving and talented girl that she was – but who was never allowed to fulfil her potential. This is a gap in our lives that can never be filled. We would ask now to be left alone to try and put the pieces of our life back together and try and look to the future.'

Milly's uncle, Brian Gilbertson, said, 'Whilst I feel some relief about the verdict today, which is tremendous news, there is so much anguish about what went on in that court and the pain that it put the family through. It was so harrowing and we felt as a family at times that we were on trial. We're just a normal family. We were and then our niece, or Sally's daughter, has been taken away from her by Bellfield – and there we were in court trying to do our best, answering to a jury exactly what went on. Bellfield decided not to give evidence and to instruct his barrister to question, it seemed, the lifestyle and everything we said, whether it was accurate and true and it made us feel as though we were on trial.'

The agonised words of the family started a heated debate in the media about the way victims and witnesses were treated in such emotive court cases. Over the next few days, the justice system as a whole came under intense scrutiny. There was immediate and widespread support for the Dowlers. The Victims' Commissioner Louise Casey said that the family's private lives were torn to shreds during the trial. 'No one in this country can think what happened to them in that courtroom was right,' said Casey, the government-appointed advocate for victims and witnesses. She said that the Lord Chief Justice should issue guidance to judges to ensure that they receive humane treatment in the witness box. She added that the Dowler experience should 'shine a light' on the way witnesses and victims are treated by the criminal justice system. 'Sadly, it's not an isolated case. I have met many families of murdered loved ones who have told me that the process has been almost as traumatic as the death itself.

'They have endured being cross-examined about the most intimate aspects of their family and private life. On top of this, they would have known that the world would read about it the next day. I am not saying that when someone is charged with a serious crime they are not entitled to a strong defence that tests the evidence in front of a jury. That is absolutely their right. But at the same time that the rich and famous obtain court orders to prevent reporting of their extramarital affairs, surely it is not too much to ask that a family who have had their lives torn apart by a murder be afforded a little privacy too? That a judge might take into account that, alongside the list of rights the defendant is granted, the family might have some rights too?' She said that the families of victims 'were not wealthy … I do sometimes wonder whether, if they were wealthy, would we treat them in the same way?'

Javed Khan, chief executive of Victim Support, said, 'The Dowlers were dragged through a court case to the point where they felt they were interrogated like criminals. They were made to feel like they were guilty of something. And that is wrong. The Crown Prosecution Service has a responsibility to step in and stop the defence barrister. It should be prepared to challenge evidence if it is damaging witnesses unnecessarily. And if it feels it does not have enough power then it must be given that power by Parliament. It looks like the defence's only line of questioning was to tear the family apart. It tried to prove that Milly was depressed and unhappy and awkward truths were forced out of her parents and sister – things that should have remained private. I'm not surprised they are upset but, unfortunately, it's a pattern being repeated every day in our courts. Defence lawyers are free to dig into the reputation of a family and make their lives a misery.'

The Chief Constable of Surrey, Mark Rowley, expressed his own views in *The Times* the day after sentence was passed. 'Sadly, her [Milly's] family now regrets supporting the prosecution and feel they have simply been pawns in a legal game. I have overseen the investigation since 2006. Having witnessed the impact of the trial on the family, I, along with the investigative team, am upset and embarrassed by how the justice system has treated them. I want to ask a simple question: rather than leaving victims and their families publicly "vilified and humiliated", can't we produce a court system in which the dignity, care and sensitivity towards them is given the same priority as a fair trial for the defendant?

'Milly's father was cross-examined on his personal life and both parents were examined on the contents of Milly's diary in a manner implying they were poor parents and that she had been unhappy. None of us can imagine how awful that must have felt but the obvious trauma is unlikely to heal for a very long time. Even some crime reporters, a hardened group, shed tears at the family's treatment ... The family's experience was so exceptionally traumatic that they now regret supporting the prosecution of Bellfield. While it is, of course, in the public interest to draw a line under an unsolved murder, I understand why they feel that way. As a chief constable, that is something I never imagined myself saying. I am left wondering why a better balance cannot be found, enabling the proper testing of witnesses without destroying them in public.'

The chairman of the Bar Council, Mr Peter Lodder QC, had differing views. Also writing in *The Times*, he said, 'There is understandable revulsion at the appalling, inhuman and murderous behaviour of Levi Bellfield. He did not acknowledge his guilt. He ran a defence that distressed his victim's family. A convicted serial killer, he even refused to attend court for his sentence. Many now liken him to an animal. In doing so, they have the moral authority that comes from knowing that he was properly represented and fairly tried, by a jury. However, that is not a licence to shoot the messenger. The case against Bellfield was not strong. It rested on the hypothesis that Milly Dowler disappeared outside his home and that this was no coincidence. But there was information that caused the police, initially, to be suspicious of Milly's father. It was cross-examination founded upon this information that distressed the Dowler family. Mark Rowley, the chief constable of Surrey, must be aware of the importance of testing in court the points that his police force's investigation raised.

'Bellfield's defence asserted that it was too easy to convict him because of his record. His instructions were to show that there were other reasons why Milly might have disappeared, as the police themselves had originally suspected. An experienced judge decided that investigation of this evidence was relevant and legitimate. The jury heard that evidence, considered it and rejected it. Justice was done.

'Jeffrey Samuels, QC, who represented Bellfield at his trial, acted in the appeal and retrial for Barry George, a man who had an obsession for celebrities and previous convictions for sexual offending. Initially convicted of the murder of Jill Dando, George was acquitted in the retrial in 2008. In that case, the media approved of the outcome. But for doing his job on behalf of Bellfield, Mr Samuels has been pilloried and his young family have suffered death threats and abuse. If a British citizen was charged with a criminal offence abroad and his lawyer was vilified for representing him, we would be outraged.

'Barristers are not permitted to turn away a case because the crime is a horrible one or because the barrister does not like the look of it. The "cab rank" rule ensures that we take the rough with the smooth. All are entitled to a proper defence and, under our justice system, up to now they have been guaranteed a capable and suitably experienced advocate to conduct it. It is all too easy to dismiss, with hindsight, the presumption of innocence that forms the bedrock of our system. Whoever the defendant, however appalling the crime, the trial process, supervised by a judge, is a strength of our system of justice.'

Roger Coe-Salazar, the CPS chief crown prosecutor in the south east, said, 'We carry our role towards victims and witnesses at the heart of what we do and we know from experience that the trial process can be a highly traumatic experience for witnesses and loved ones. The adversarial nature of our criminal trial system in this country is designed to test the evidence given by witnesses, be they for the prosecution or defence, so as to ensure safe conviction and acquittal of the innocent. We must recognise that there are some aspects of the trial, in particular in cross-examination, which no amount of general foresight can ever prepare someone for.'

The CPS was legally required to disclose to the defence evidence obtained during the initial police investigation and 'even in such emotive moments we cannot lose sight of a fundamental principle within our legal system that a defendant should be able to advance his defence before a jury. Once we became aware of the actual nature of the defence that was going to be put forward and the likely evidence that would be advanced to support the defence theory we applied for reporting restrictions on the cross-examination. The judge, in balancing the representations of the prosecution with the interests of open justice, refused the prosecution's application. During the course of Sally Dowler's cross-examination the prosecution did object to questioning by the defence wherever we legitimately could. After witnessing the distress the experience caused Mrs Dowler we decided not to call Milly's sister Gemma to give evidence. It is a testament to the Dowler family's fortitude that they supported the prosecution of Levi Bellfield for the abominable crime he committed. I know they feel today that the jury trial process has let them down, but I hope that in the future the pain and anguish they are presently feeling will be somewhat diluted as a result of the convictions secured today.'

Marsha McDonnell's uncle, Shane, commented on the issue of the cross-examination. 'As much as we respect the absolute need for a defence action to be as strong as possible, we would question the manner in which this particular case was handled by Jeffrey Samuels for Carter Moore Solicitors. Not only were they dealing with a convicted murderer but a man with a very clear proven history of manipulation, hatred, lies and deceit, a man known to have no remorse whatsoever and a man who is known to relish bringing more pain to the families of his victims wherever possible.'

Jeremy Moore was managing partner of Carter Moore and head of the serious and organised crime team. He said it was the 'cornerstone of our justice system that every defendant, however unpalatable, has the right to have his defence put – and to a fair trial. In order to ensure a fair trial, it is the duty of defence lawyers to test the prosecution case by the cross-examination of prosecution witnesses along relevant lines of questioning. In this particular case, material was disclosed to the defence which, while being of a sensitive nature, was highly relevant to some of the issues in the trial and it became necessary and appropriate to put these matters to certain prosecution witnesses. These matters were put as economically as possible and in no way gratuitously and, had either the prosecution or learned judge considered any such questioning to be irrelevant or inappropriate, it would not have been allowed.'

CHAPTER 12

Surrey police's handling of the case raised as much concern as had the Dowlers' treatment in court. So much so that Surrey's assistant chief constable Jerry Kirby admitted 'mistakes were made'. As the trial ended, the force formally apologised for their 'poor initial response' at the beginning of the £6 million investigation into Milly's murder.

He said the force had 'agonised' over whether their failure to follow up a number of early leads could have contributed to the murders of two young women. 'In long-running investigations like this, questions are often raised as to whether the perpetrator [could have been caught] sooner and whether any action on our part could have prevented further offences. With the benefit of hindsight, there are aspects of the investigation we would have handled differently. It was a poor initial response.'

An obvious failure was in the response to the call from Rachel Cowles' mother. She notified the police that her daughter had been approached by a stranger in a red car. The encounter took place near where Milly was abducted and just one day earlier, but, while the call was logged, the information was never passed to the incident room. Rachel was not interviewed and no statement was taken. Three years later, Mrs Cowles made contact with the police again. Even then she had to call twice and write a letter before there was a follow-up.

Another missed opportunity involved house-to-house enquiries and the flat at Collingwood Place. Bellfield had been using the address for credit card frauds around the time Milly vanished and police later became aware of those offences. Yet Mr Kirby said Bellfield did not become a suspect and his flat was not visited until 2004, when Metropolitan police investigating the murder of Amelie put forward his name as a 'person of interest'. Mr Kirby said, 'Again, with the benefit of hindsight, we accept the house-to-house enquiries should have been done differently.' These enquiries, he admitted were 'extensive but not exhaustive. Given the locality of Collingwood Place, we accept we should have been more exhaustive. That said, even if Levi Bellfield himself had answered the door, there's nothing to suggest, at that time, we would have identified him as a suspect.'

DCI Woodall was in court for every day of the trial and her conduct was praised by the Dowler family. She said, 'It has been a long and challenging fight to obtain justice for Milly and I hope that this verdict, proving who was responsible for her murder, will enable the Dowler family to return to a private life once again. This has been an incredibly difficult process for them and it is important to remember who has been on trial here – it is not the grieving and loving family of a 13-year-old girl. The Surrey police investigation into Milly's murder, Operation Ruby, has been long, complicated and challenging for everyone involved and it has taken many years of painstaking, detective work to reach this conclusion. Unlike most similar crimes, there were no witnesses, no immediate suspects and no forensic material to work with. Officers and staff have worked tirelessly on this investigation – some from the beginning of the case up to today – to find out who killed Milly. Surrey police would never give up on solving this case – however long it took – it was too important.

'There are no words to adequately describe Levi Bellfield – this is a man who kidnapped a young girl while she was walking home from school, murdered her, removed all of her belongings and left her somewhere that she would not be found. Milly's family have been tortured by the actions of this devious and dangerous man, who intimidates partners, family and acquaintances and is adept at covering his tracks. Throughout the investigation, Bellfield refused to speak to the police and has never showed a shred of remorse. He has not only robbed the Dowler family of their daughter and put them through almost a decade of hell, but he has also put them through the ordeal of a lengthy trial.'

During the hunt for Milly and her killer, there had been 3,500 house-to-house enquiries, 35 miles of waterway had been searched, 5,600 statements had been taken and there had been 256 people 'of potential interest' to the police. There had been 'sightings' of Milly in places as far apart as Fiji and the Bilbao car ferry. There were also reports that Surrey police had bugged Bob Dowler's home and his car at one stage, although the force refused to comment. They would only point out that '98 per cent of victims are known to the people who murder them'.

The family of Marsha McDonnell were also concerned about the Surrey police investigation. In a statement issued on behalf of her family, her uncle Shane McDonnell said, 'Our first thoughts are with Milly Dowler's family. We hope that, even after all this time, this conviction brings them the same small amount of closure as Bellfield's conviction in 2008 brought to our family. We were appalled, along with the rest of the nation, at the disgraceful treatment they were subjected to in court and we hope they are still able to salvage some good from today's result. Our hearts go out to them. Following the progress of this trial, the question never far from our minds was: "Could anything have been done differently, following Milly's disappearance and subsequent murder, that could have prevented Bellfield from being able to go on to commit the further heinous crimes that have blighted so many lives and taken from us our beloved Marsha?" One only has to listen to the testimony of Emma Mills to realise how close Bellfield could have come to being apprehended much sooner than he was. It may have taken only one more, small event – such as the CCTV footage of the red car or indeed a routine visit by the police – to have given Ms Mills the confidence to allow her to voice her suspicions. While we commend Surrey police for the work performed in bringing about today's conviction, we cannot with clear conscience do so without calling upon the relevant authority to instigate a very precise review of all that went on in that initial investigation by the Surrey force into Milly's disappearance and subsequent murder.

'Whatever terms of reference the review is conducted under, we would strongly request that the following are given full consideration:

'1. Was the investigation flawed to such an extent that, in its inability to identify Bellfield as a prime suspect, it can be held accountable in any way for the failure to prevent the murder of two young innocent women and the attempted murder of a third?

'2. If this review does identify errors and mistakes, what measures can be established to ensure that the same errors and mistakes are never made again?

'It is always easy in hindsight to make judgements showing how things could have been done differently. However, from facts that have emerged throughout this trial, it would appear there are some fundamental procedures that need clarification to show whether they were performed correctly, effectively or at all. While we wish to see a review into every aspect of that investigation, we would identify the following three as being of paramount importance:

'1. Why was it that no successful visit was made to Bellfield's apartment or the occupation of that apartment established when it is known that it was close to where Milly disappeared?

'2. After Milly's disappearance, when was the call reporting the attempted abduction of Rachel Cowles only the day before followed up? And what prevented that call from becoming a priority line of enquiry once Milly went missing?

'3. When did the investigation first become aware of the CCTV footage of the red Daewoo and could this have been identified any sooner?

'Of course, no review will ever bring back our loved ones or take away the mental and physical anguish suffered by his victims but it may help to bring about practices that will ensure, if the review identifies any shortcomings, that similar errors or mistakes can never happen again. We congratulate prosecution counsel Brian Altman QC on securing this further and necessary conviction against Levi Bellfield. We hope that the whole world now sees him for exactly what he is. We hope that we will never again have to listen to the web of lies, deceit and denials that he likes to spin. We also acknowledge all those other victims of Bellfield's violence, those who have never been able to have their day in court. We hope that they can now derive some satisfaction from today's result and, as with us, hope that this is the last the world has to hear of him. It is satisfying to know that this man can bring no further hurt to the world.'

Amelie's mother, Dominique, told ITV news, 'It's true there is the question that, if the same thorough investigation had been carried out in the case of Milly, then Marsha and Amelie would still be alive. That question remains. For the time being I don't dare think about it too much. It stirs up so many things to be regretted and alas that won't bring Amelie back.'

Rachel Cowles was unhappy about certain elements of the trial in which she had featured so prominently. 'I feel very lucky that I got away. When it came out about Milly, it really hit me that it could have been me. I genuinely felt that I could put the experience to good use to help find Milly's killer. I am very angry and hurt, and I feel I have been robbed of justice. [When the jury was discharged] I burst into tears. This whole thing has been very difficult and frightening, both recognising Bellfield in court and giving evidence. I just want to be able to draw a line in the sand and move on.'

For her part, Rachel's mother said, 'It had to be more than a coincidence that Rachel was approached on the road where Milly went missing. Two girls, in two days – surely there had to be a connection? The police weren't taking us seriously.'

No one, apart from Levi Bellfield, will ever know how many women he attacked during the years he roamed the streets and nightclubs. Colin Sutton headed the Met's hunt and was instrumental in pointing Surrey police in his direction. He wrote in *The Times* as Bellfield prepared to return to his cell in Wakefield prison. Summing the violent thug up perfectly, he said, 'He is charming and vicious, intelligent but uneducated, cunning and reckless. The combination of these competing traits with his voracious sexual appetite and his utter contempt for women and girls led to a long line of girlfriends and partners, many of them bearing his children. He believed that he could have any woman he chose. So the women who dared to rebuff the great Levi Bellfield were attacked.

'Bellfield is not just a killer. The killings were simply inevitable conclusions to everyday episodes of sexually driven arrogance and a complete disregard for authority and normal behaviour. All that matters to Bellfield is Bellfield. Serial offenders often lead a double life: friends and family are shocked when their crimes come to light. Nobody who knew Bellfield was surprised by what he had done, just that it took him so long to be caught.'